ADAM SMITH SPEAKS TO OUR TIMES

ADAM SMITH SPEAKS TO OUR TIMES

A Study of His Ethical Ideas

By

ROBERT BRANK FULTON

Author of "Original Marxism — Estranged Offspring"

THE CHRISTOPHER PUBLISHING HOUSE
BOSTON, U.S.A.

To

FOUR PARENTS

My own, for their confidence and support, while yet in this life, during the early stages of research;

Those gained through marriage, for their encouragement, especially by taking into their home the writer and his entire family during the leave from teaching when the manuscript was hammered into shape.

TABLE OF CONTENTS

CHAPTER FOUR

CHAPTER FIVE

ACKNOWLEDGMENTS

Appreciation is gladly expressed to the following publishers for permission to quote from one or more of their publications: the Baker Library of the Harvard Graduate School of Business Administration; the British Academy; *The Philosophical Review*, Cornell University; Thomas Nelson and Sons (for the National Council of Churches with reference to the Revised Standard Version of the Bible); Random House, Inc. (for a Modern Library volume); the World Council of Churches, Inc. (including the Division of World Mission and Evangelism); and Yale University Press.

Thanks are also due, and herewith expressed, to the New York City, Princeton University, and Yale University Libraries for the use of their resources and facilities, to Inter-American University of Puerto Rico for the leave of absence for preparing the manuscript, and to several teachers and counselors whose advice has been invaluable but whose names are omitted to relieve them from any responsibility for ideas here set forth.

PREFACE

Why another book on Adam Smith? Isn't the thought of the old gentleman (do we ever think of him as youthful?) pretty well covered already? Doesn't he belong quite precisely in his recognized historical niche as the father of economic individualism, the conventional author of "The Wealth of Nations", the conservative advocate of "laissez-faire"?

My answers to these questions would have been the obvious ones and I would not have been involved in this project had it not been for the following experiences:

1. When I was a graduate student in a course on the History of Economic Thought, the professor opened his first lecture with the intellectually startling words, "Gentlemen, I am both a Smithian and a Marxian and I am not a split-personality"; and the course demonstrated the possibility of maintaining such a position.

2. Somewhat later, when I was enrolled as a Ph.D. student in Christian Ethics, my advisor suggested the comparison of Smith and Marx with specific reference to their religious presuppositions; and my dissertation subject became "The Problem of Religious Assumptions in the Systems of Adam Smith and Karl Marx", involving a more thorough study of each than I had ever made before.

3. Teaching a course, somewhat later, in a Chinese university, on the History of Economic Thought I

found myself more and more in agreement with the
words in the introduction to the Modern Library Edition of "The Wealth of Nations":

> "Adam Smith was in his own day and in his
> own way something of a revolutionary. His doc-
> trine revolutionized European society as surely as
> Marx's in a later epoch."[1]

However, I would extend this implication of freshness
of approach to include his whole view on life, not just
his economic ideas.

4. Study of Smith's writings, both for purposes of
the dissertation and the teaching in China, and since
then in relation to other courses in the fields of religion and philosophy, has convinced me of the integral
relation of his ethical views to his approach to economic and political matters; and it has led, also, to a
growing sense of his right to greater recognition as an
ethicist than he normally receives today and of the
relevance of his views to the effort to face certain 20th
century problems as well as those of the 18th.

While the material collected for the dissertation has
been made considerable use of, the present work has
involved a thorough rewriting, with both additions
and omissions, with a view to focusing on the central
purpose — the exploration of the significance of Smith's
ideas as we deal with some of the crucial ethical problems of our day.

It should be added that the extensive use of quotations, some of them quite lengthy, is deliberate — the
decision to do so having been made for the following
reasons:

1. "The Theory of Moral Sentiments", from which
most of the quotations come, is so very difficult to lo-

cate for reference purpose, being long out of print, that
making the pertinent passages available has seemed
essential — long paraphrases being apt to raise the
question of possible, however unintentional, misinter-
pretation.

2. It has seemed well to make the relevant material
from "An Inquiry into the Nature and Causes of the
Wealth of Nations" also thus readily available as not
all potential readers of this volume will have even
Smith's better known work at hand.

3. Apparent in at least some of the quotations is
what the Messrs. Gide and Rist call Smith's "supreme
literary charm",[2] an aspect of his writing which probably has added considerably to his influence among
his readers.

REFERENCES

[1] Smith, Adam, "An Inquiry into the Nature and Causes of the
Wealth of Nations", New York, The Modern Library, 1937, p. x. The
introduction is by Max Lerner.

[2] Gide, Charles and Rist, Charles, "A History of Economic Doctrines", New York, Boston, etc., D. C. Heath and Company, no date,
p. 51.

Adam Smith Speaks to Our Times

CHAPTER ONE

SOME BASIC ETHICAL PROBLEMS

We live in a day when ethical problems are far more sharply in focus than accepted ways of dealing with them — the "acids of modernity" that Walter Lippmann called so vividly to our attention some thirty years ago in "A Preface to Morals" having continued to dissolve the confidence of many in concepts and practices previously taken almost for granted.

There is, for example, the old yet markedly contemporary problem of *the relationship of the individual and society.* Is there an irreconcilable conflict between them requiring an ultimate choice between more or less rugged individualism and collectivism? Growing out of the first is the problem of *the relationship of private enterprise and government activity* in the economic sphere. Are these fundamentally alternatives — the one being advanced at the expense of the other? Akin, yet so full of explosive possibilities as to be almost in a class by itself, is the problem of *international relations.* Are the interests of individual states incompatible with the pursuit of global well-being? Permeating all these, as well as being a question with major dimensions itself, is the problem of *justice and love.* Is it a matter of "either-or" between them, or are

they capable of being brought into a creative syn-
thesis?

Doubtless all would agree that these are indeed real
problems — age-old but also present-day in so vital a
sense that on at least an approximation of an adequate
solution for each may hang not only the welfare but
the very survival of our civilization. But why call them
all "ethical"? Are we not thus confusing categories
that ought to be kept separate — economic, political,
legal, philosophic, religious? Unquestionably there
are real values in maintaining distinctions between
such aspects of human relationships; but it would also
seem to be worthwhile to examine the common ground
among them and to do this by focusing our attention
on what are here termed their ethical dimensions.

This brings us unavoidably to a consideration of
what "ethics" — and more specifically "Christian ethics"
— is to be assumed to mean in this study. The word
is sometimes used, as any dictionary indicates, as the
virtual equivalent of "mores" or social customs; but
in its fuller sense it carries with it a positive sense of
"oughtness", of what ought to be. However, it is "what
ought to be", not in some fanciful world of the imagination, but in actual relation to "what is". In other
words, it involves the possible change of "what is" into
a more praiseworthy form, whether by gradual or more
rapid, perhaps even revolutionary, development.

This obviously presupposes, whether or not explicitly recognized, a criterion of judgment. It may be, as
in philosophy, reason alone; or it may, as in theology,
include not only reason but whatever is accepted as
divine revelation. Also, the word "ethics" carries with
it in at least some usage the aspect of action as well as
that of formulation — the endeavor to realize in prac-

tice what has been conceived of as right, including the
choice of methods to be used.

May we, then, at least as a hypothesis for this study,
think of *ethics* as involving *the disciplined effort of
mind and will to formulate and carry out what are
considered to be the implications of either reason alone
(philosophical ethics) or of reason and accepted revelation (theological ethics), in human relations?* We
will be considering in Chapter Four the relation of
Smith's thought to Christianity, so the question of the
specific content of Christian ethics will be dealt with
in that context.

Clearly, then, in the light of such a concept the problems listed earlier in this brief chapter come under the
heading of "ethical", at least to a considerable extent;
and anyone who has anything significant to say with
reference to the effort to solve them deserves a hear-
ing. It is the writer's conviction that Adam Smith does
indeed have much to say in these regards that is worthy
of serious attention. We will be dealing with his specific contributions in these areas in Chapter Five; but
it seems well first to renew our awareness of the historical framework of, and the main aspects of, his life
and work in the categories of the chief characteristics
of his times and the main facts of his life (Chapter
Two), his over-all system of thought (Chapter Three),
and his relationship, in life and thought, to Christianity (Chapter Four).

CHAPTER TWO

SMITH AND HIS TIMES

It has become a commonplace to say that to understand fully a man's thought one must know something
of its historical context. This is not to subscribe to any
rigidly deterministic method of interpretation, but it
is to emphasize the conditioning influence of the general "milieu", especially the "climate of opinion" of the
period.[1] Fortunately, the 18th century is near enough
to us to be relatively familiar in its general outline, but
some of its more distinctive characteristics may well
be called to mind, especially those that influenced
Smith strongly, either directly or indirectly; and it
seems well to reverse the order of the chapter's title
and look first at "the times" before coming to Smith
himself.

A. *Some Features of the 18th Century*

It was the "Age of the Enlightenment" — at least (so
they were convinced) of the minds of the "Philosophes" in France and their counterparts in England, as
well as those in other parts of Europe and the American colonies. The list of great names among Smith's
philosophical contemporaries includes Montesquieu,
Voltaire, Rousseau, Diderot, Helvetius, Baron d'Hol-
bach, Turgot, Quesnay and Condorcet in France;
Locke, Hume, Bolingbroke, Ferguson, Price and
Priestly in the British Isles; Leibnitz, Lessing, Herder
and Goethe in Germany; and, in the New World, Jef-

ferson and Franklin.[2] "The philosophical empire was
an international domain of which France was but the
mother country and Paris the capital. Go where you
like — England, Holland, Italy, Spain, America —
everywhere you meet them, Philosophers speaking the
same language, sustained by the same climate of opinion." And Carl L. Becker continues:

> "They are of all countries and of none, having
> openly declared their allegiance to mankind, desir-
> ing nothing so much as to be counted 'among the
> small number of those who by their intelligence
> and their works have merited well of humanity'.
> They are citizens of the world, the emancipated
> ones, looking out upon a universe seemingly brand
> new because so freshly flooded with light, a uni-
> verse in which everything worth attending to is
> visible, and everything visible is seen to be un-
> blurred and wonderfully simple after all, and evi-
> dently intelligible to the human mind — the mind
> of Philosophers."[3]

1. Reason and Nature

When we think of the chief characteristics of the
period we come first to the emphasis placed on reason
and the rational method, generally held to be diamet-
rically opposed to the traditionalism and dogmatic
method associated with medieval ecclesiasticism. In
the words of Dean Inge, it was at this time that, "West-
ern Europe began to dream of an approaching millen-
nium without miracle, to be gradually ushered in under the faculty which was called Reason."[4] In the light
of this new movement of thought, the leaders dis-
covered much around about them of which they did

not approve; and their resulting criticisms were vigorous and often vitriolic. As another student of the period says:

> "There was a widespread feeling that many of the ideas and institutions of the eighteenth century had survived their usefulness and the trend of thought was to subject the whole field of political and social life to scrutiny and criticism . . . The prevailing 'motif' of the whole movement was towards moral, political and social justification, but a justification which must be established by reason, not by faith or authority."[5]

With dogma and custom no longer available as rationally acceptable standards of judgment for them, the philosophers had to look elsewhere; and by common consent the new criterion became Nature with a capital "N". Its content, though not always precisely the same, generally consisted of ideas coming from Greco-Roman concepts of natural law (the "ius naturale" of the Stoics, especially), with emphasis, coming from "natural theology", on the basic identity of the law of Nature with the Divine law.[6] Once more to quote Becker:

> "Nature and natural law — what magic these words held for the philosophical century! Enter that country by any door you like, you are at once aware of its pervasive power . . . The ideas, the customs, the institutions of men, if ever they are to attain perfection, must obviously be in accord with those laws which 'nature reveals at all times, to all men'."[7]

Of interest at this point is the evidence, not yet given the thorough treatment it would seem to merit, of the influence on 18th century European thinkers of Chinese philosophy and civilization with the tremendous emphasis of the principal Chinese tradition on seeking to understand and conform to Nature, man finding in this way his fulfillment in all aspects of life — philosophical, political, ethical, and artistic.[8]

2. Individualism

In addition to the admiration of reason and the rational method, with Nature as the touchstone, was the strong emphasis placed on the individual. The form which it took was largely worked out by Locke and was the result of the rationalistic method he employed in his thought-system, with concern to analyze each problem or situation to the point where its ultimate elements could be identified. After developing this approach to an understanding of the period an able interpreter writes:

> "Just as he (Locke) attempted to separate the understanding into psychic elements and explain the whole by the parts, so he conceived of social phenomena in terms of isolated individuals, considered as the basic elements of which society is only a more complex derivative. From this individualism were derived the characteristic social and political problems of the century."[9]

With the individual so central as the pivotal unit, it was naturally most important to examine him carefully to find out how he behaves in various circumstances and how he may best be led to conform to natural law. Society was conceived, thus, as a union of individuals,

whether based on the contract theory in one form or
another or regarded as more or less spontaneous in origin. "And so the determination of the characteristics
of the isolated individual — his motives to activity, his
selfish or neutral or benevolent affections and the like
— became of supreme importance."[10]

The impact of this emphasis, shared by so many in
the 18th century, on the thought and institutions of
the West has been very great, as we know, right down
to the present.

3. The Challenge of the Social Interpretation

The forces of extreme rationalism and individualism were not allowed to go unchallenged in the latter
part of the century, however — the most significant
counter-claims being made by the school of Shaftesbury, Hutcheson, Butler, and Hume with their special
emphases, respectively, on propriety and a sense of
fellowship, benevolence, conscience, and "the principle
of sympathy or communication".[11] Especially important for Smith was the work of his close friend David
Hume, whose emphasis has been thus interpreted:

> "Hume's adoption of the 'principle of sympathy
> or communication' as the basis of the moral experi-
> ence is one of the most significant facts in eight-
> eenth-century ethics, because as used by him it
> really amounted to an abandonment of the indi-
> vidualistic way of stating the ethical problem . . .
> It implied that, on the contrary, the true explana-
> tion of the moral experience is to be found in the
> association of individuals with one another; i.e.,
> that we must recognize the social as well as the in-
> dividual factor in the development of the moral
> consciousness."[12]

So, the individual was placed in a distinctly societal context, at least by some 18th century thinkers before Smith.

4. The Continuing Influence of Christianity

Despite frequent attacks of the "Philosophers" on ecclesiastical dogma and institutions, there was a marked carry-over of Christian influences. As an illustration of this we may compare what have been called "the essential articles of the religion of the Enlightenment"[13] — that is, its basic presuppositions, which were taken for granted — with certain Christian doctrines as set forth in selections from Scriptural passages:

1. "Man is not natively depraved."

1. "And God created man in his own image . . . And God saw everything that he had made, and behold, it was very good." (Genesis 1:27,31)

2. "The end of life is life itself, the good life on earth instead of the beatific life after death."

2. "I am come that they might have life, and that they might have it more abundantly." (John 10:10) "Thy kingdom come. Thy will be done." (Matthew 6:10)

3. "Man is capable, guided solely by the light of reason and experience, of perfecting the good life on earth."

3. "Work out your own salvation . . . (Philippians 2:12) "Be ye therefore perfect . . ." (Matthew 5:48)

4. "The first and essential condition of the good life on earth is the freeing of men's minds from the bonds of ignorance and superstition, and of their bodies from the arbitrary oppression of the constituted authorities."

4. "Ye shall know the truth and the truth shall make you free." (John 8:32) "He hath sent me to proclaim release to the captives, and recovery of the sight of the blind, to set at liberty them that are bruised" ("to set free the oppressed" — Moffatt translation). (Luke 4:18)

So, in spite of all the open opposition to organized Christianity *per se* there were striking similarities between the thought of "the Enlightenment" and certain ideas and assumptions that had been part of Christianity for centuries. What we seem to have, then, is not a group of completely new ideas but a choice (conscious or unconscious) of certain Christian concepts with the omission of others.[14]

Of the entire century it has been said, "Its characteristic note is not a disillusioned indifference, but the eager didactic impulse to set things right"; and, continues the same penetrating student of the period, its characteristic words, such as "bienfaisance" and "humanité" were "coined by the Philosophers to express in secular terms the Christian ideal of service".[15]

5. *Other Factors*

Even such a brief treatment of Smith's environment should also include mention of such facts as the following:

a. that the preceding epoch — which was not yet dead — had been one of dynastic-aristocratic nationalism, a mercantilist age in which aggregate rather than per capita wealth was the national economic goal;

b. that it was an age in which factories were tiny and machines hardly more than machine tools;

c. that political democracy was still in its early stages, with the control of government largely in the hands of the landed gentry;

d. that education was both in fact and in aim the privilege of the few, with any but the most elemental liberties pretty much limited to their circle.[16]

It was against such limitations of privilege and control that Smith was fighting throughout his life, with especially telling blows dealt in "The Wealth of Nations"; and it is well to keep this fact in mind if there is any truth in the statement that if we wish to understand any forceful writer we must find out what he is reacting against.[17]

B. A Brief Sketch of Smith's Life

Such were some of the major characteristics of the "milieu" of Adam Smith, whose life of study, teaching and writing was spent during the central years of the century (1723-90).

1. 1723-47

Born into a Scottish Presbyterian family, Smith was reared by his mother, the daughter of a well-to-do landed proprietor. Of her we read that "contemporary accounts agree that she was deeply religious", and the writer continues:

> "Her judgment in the affairs of life which came under her attention was sound and at the same time charitable. There could have been few better mothers for a fatherless boy."[18]

The same biographer speaks also of the "particularly close and tender tie between him (Smith) and his mother",[19] who lived almost as long as her son. His father, who died before he was born, had served as "Writer to the Signet, Judge Advocate for Scotland, and Comptroller of the Customs in the Kirkcaldy dis-

trict" and also for a time as Private Secretary to the
Scottish minister, the Earl of Loudon; and Rae con-
siders it likely that the elder Mr. Smith was, like the
Earl, "a zealous Whig and Presbyterian".[20]

His childhood and youth seem to have been relatively normal and unspectacular (except for his being
stolen for a few hours by a gypsy while still an infant),
though he early showed real prowess as a student,
being ready to enter Glasgow College by his four-
teenth year. The college was having at that time an
"intellectual awakening" — the result mainly of the
teaching of three professors — Alexander Dunlop
(Greek), Robert Simson (Mathematics) and above all,
Francis Hutcheson, "a thinker of great original power,
and an unrivalled academic lecturer".[21]

> "Whatever he touched upon, he treated . . .
> with a certain freshness and decided originality
> which must have provoked even the dullest to
> some reflection, and in a bracing spirit of intel-
> lectual liberty which it was strength and life for
> the young mind to breathe."[22]

Small wonder that Smith referred to him later as "the
never-to-be-forgotten Hutcheson" and that between
them there developed one of those great teacher-stu-
dent relationships which result in oneness of essential
spirit without destroying the independent creativeness
of the student. Speaking of them as closely akin in
their basic approach to life, another biographer of
Smith writes:

> "With Hutcheson and Smith it was a real reli-
> gion to see that society should be better governed;
> they made it the supreme object of their lives to
> increase the happiness of mankind by diffusing

useful truths and exposing mischievous errors. In
the scope of his philosophy, in temper and practical aim, Smith may be called the spiritual de-
scendant of Hutcheson."[23]

It was he (Hutcheson), incidentally, who coined the
famous phrase "the greatest happiness of the greatest
number" as the expression of a social goal.[24]

It was through Hutcheson, too, that Smith first came
into contact with David Hume, who was to become
his "dearest friend" and who reportedly presented the
young student with a copy of his "Treatise of Human
Nature" in appreciation of the abstract of it which
Smith had prepared.[25]

Thus two of the greatest influences on his thought —
the systems of Hutcheson and Hume — had come into
Smith's life before his eighteenth year. That of Grotius
and Pufendorf, with their great emphasis on Natural
Law, also began during this college period and was
likewise to have great effect on all his work.[26]

Receiving, as a reward for his scholarship, an appointment to one of the Snell "exhibitions" at Balliol
College, Oxford — founded to prepare students "to
enter holy orders and return to serve the Church in
Scotland"[27] — Smith spent the next six years in England. There is no direct indication of his own intention
at the time of accepting the appointment, but he made
no effort to enter the ministry at the close of his period
of study. Oxford was at a very low point educationally
at this time — Smith writing later, "In the University
of Oxford, the greater part of the public professors
have, for these many years, given up even the pretense
of teaching".[28] However, his time was by no means
wasted, for he was enough of a student to be able to
do his own work, taking advantage of the library

which was strong in the classics of Greek and Latin,
Italian, French, and English literature; and he worked
on the improvement of his own English style as well.[29]

2. 1747-64

After two years without employment, Smith became
a public lecturer in Edinburgh, on English literature
and criticism, meeting with considerable success; and
he soon added a course on economics also.

Then in 1750, at the age of twenty-seven, he was
appointed to the chair of Logic and Rhetoric at Glasgow, succeeding his old teacher, John Loudon.[30] He
carried on at the same time the work of the chair of
Moral Philosophy due to the illness of the incumbent
(Professor Craigie); and when the latter died, Smith
was elected to be his successor, thus occupying the
chair once held by his revered teacher Francis Hutcheson. He held this position until his resignation to take
up other work thirteen years later.

One of his favorite students, who was later an active
colleague, John Millar, prepared the following descrip-
tion, which is quoted in full because of the light it
throws on the general scheme of Smith's thought:

> "His course of lectures was divided into four
> parts. The first contained natural theology, in
> which he considered the proofs of the being and
> attributes of God, and those principles of the hu-
> man mind upon which religion is founded.
>
> "The second comprehended ethics, strictly so
> called, and consisted chiefly of the doctrines
> which he afterwards published in his 'Theory of
> Moral Sentiments'.
>
> "In the third part he treated at more length of

that branch of morality which relates to justice, and which, being susceptible of precise and accurate rules, is for that reason capable of a full and particular explanation. Upon this subject he followed the plan that seems to be suggested by Montesquieu, endeavoring to trace the gradual progress of jurisprudence, both public and private, from the rudest to the most refined ages, and to point out the effects of those arts which contribute to subsistence and to the accumulation of property, in producing corresponding improvements or alterations in law and government. This important branch of his labours he also intended to give to the public; but this intention, which is mentioned in the conclusion of the 'Theory of Moral Sentiments', he did not live to fulfill.

"In the last of his lectures he examined those political regulations which are founded, not upon the principle of justice but that of expediency, and which are calculated to increase the riches, the power, and the prosperity of a state. Under this view he considered the political institutions relating to commerce, to finances, to ecclesiastical and military establishments. What he delivered on those subjects contained the substance of the work he afterwards published under the title of 'An Inquiry into the Nature and Causes of the Wealth of Nations'."[31]

A copy of the third and fourth sections of these lectures, as taken down by one of Smith's students, turned up over a hundred years after his death, as pointed out by Cannan in his introduction to the volume known as "Lectures of Adam Smith".

Smith was apparently popular as a teacher, with an intellectually stimulating effect on his students; his opinions became subjects of general discussion in the town as well as the college, and "stucco busts of him appeared in the booksellers' windows and the very peculiarities of his voice and pronunciation received the homage of imitation".[32]

Even before the publication of "The Theory of Moral Sentiments" in 1759, Smith was well-known among intellectual and political leaders; and after the publication his was a name to conjure with. One evidence of the book's success is a letter from Hume conveying "the melancholy news that your book has been very unfortunate, for the public seems disposed to applaud it extremely!"[33] — as did Hume himself.

3. 1764-90

One of the effects of the "Theory" was the offer a few years later of the position of tutor to the young Duke of Buccleugh (at a salary of £300 a year with traveling expenses while abroad and a pension of £300 a year thereafter for the rest of his life) which Smith accepted. He resigned his professorship at Glasgow early in 1864 and soon set out on his travels with his young charge.[34] During the next two years on the continent Smith made the most of his opportunities and became personally acquainted with such "philosophes" as Turgot, Quesnay, Helvétius, and Voltaire. For the last mentioned he had especially great admiration — probably, judging from Smith's own character, for such qualities as are emphasized in the following characterization:

"Voltaire was an optimist, although not a naive one. He was the defender of causes, and not of lost causes — a crusader pledged to recover the holy places of the true faith, the religion of humanity. Voltaire, skeptic? — strange misconception! On the contrary, a man of faith, an apostle who fought the good fight, tireless to the end, writing seventy volumes to convey the truth that was to make us free."[35]

Smith was a regular guest in the most famous literary salons in Paris, due partly to his own reputation and partly to the influence of his friend Hume, then "king of the philosophes".[36] However, the two years abroad were by no means a literary and social lark, for the experience gave him opportunities for first-hand study of social and economic conditions on the continent, especially in France. That he made good use of them is borne out by frequent comments in his later work.

The next ten years were spent partly in London and partly in Scotland and were used chiefly in the preparation of his famous "Inquiry into the Nature and Causes of the Wealth of Nations", which appeared in the same year as the American "Declaration of Independence" — 1776. (That he was concerned with what was going on across the Atlantic and that he was fearless in accepting and stating the conclusions to which his researches and thinking pointed out is made clear by passages which will be dealt with in Chapter Five.) This work had been promised in the last paragraph of the "Theory" and thus in Smith's mind formed a part of the general system of thought that he had developed in his lectures — a connection which he confirmed in his preface to the 1790 edition of the "Theory".[37]   It was well received and widely read; and within a decade many of its recommendations were being carried out by the government, especially under the sponsorship of William Pitt, who "always confessed himself one of Smith's most convinced disciples" — Smith's influence over him being dramatically indicated in the following story included in Rae's biography:

> "They (Pitt and Smith) met repeatedly, but they met on one occasion, of which recollection has been preserved, at Dundas's house on Wimbledon Green — Addington, Wilberforce, and Grenville being also of the company; and it is said that when Smith, who was one of the last guests to arrive, entered the room, the whole company rose from their seats to receive him and remained standing. 'Be seated, gentlemen', said Smith. 'No,' replied Pitt; 'we will stand till you are first seated, for we are all your scholars'!"[38]

And in a recent essay on Smith's work we read:

> "The influence of the 'Wealth of Nations' on political policy and legislative action was notable. The book early became the 'vade mecum' of every aspiring publicist. Buckle has industriously located thirty-seven instances between 1783 and 1800 in which the 'Parliamentary History' records an appeal to Adam Smith's authority."[39]

A little less than two years after the publication, Smith was appointed one of the Commissioners of Customs in Scotland, "an express recognition on the part of the Premier of the public value of Smith's work, and the more honorable because rendered to a political opponent who had condemned important parts of the ministerial policy — their American policy, for example — in his recent work".[40]   He took up his residence then at Edinburgh, where he did his work (so similar to that of his father's), spending his leisure time with his mother, his friends, and his books — "Smith's three great joys".[41] Hume had died in 1776, but many other friends and admirers made their way to Smith's home, and he was consulted by government officials and others on various questions of public policy.   His "alma mater" also honored him by appointing him Lord Rector of the University of Glasgow, an action he deeply appreciated.[42]

He had intended to write a book on jurisprudence (the third section of his Glasgow lectures), as already noted, but time proved too short for him to accomplish this plan.   However, he did revise his "Theory of Moral Sentiments" in the last year of his life, including a number of new passages, of which one has consider-able bearing on our inquiry.   Referring to those who have been unjustly punished, he wrote:

"Religion can alone afford them any effectual comfort.   She also can tell them that it is of little importance what men may think of their conduct while the all-seeing Judge of the word approves of it.   She alone can present to them a view of another world — a world of more candour, human-ity, and justice than the present, where their in-nocence is in due time to be declared and their virtue to be finally rewarded, and the same great principle which can alone strike terror into trium-

phant vice affords the only effectual consolation
of disgraced and insulted innocence."[43]

And the chief biographer adds, "These words, written
on the eve of his own death, show that he died as he
lived, in the full faith of those doctrines of natural
religion which he publicly taught."[44]

One of his last acts — understandable, yet most
regrettable — was the destruction, with the help of two
friends, of the greater part of his unpublished manuscripts; these sixteen volumes were described by his
friend and first biographer, Dugald Stewart, as probably containing "the letters on rhetoric, which he read
at Edinburgh in the year 1748, and of the lectures on
natural religion and on jurisprudence, which formed
part of his course at Glasgow".[45]

Summary estimates of Smith and his work by three
keen students — a Frenchman, an American, and a
fellow Scotsman — may well bring this sketch to a
close. Writes Delatour in his biography:

> "One should see in Adam Smith not only the
> scholar and philosopher who has cleared up the
> laws of things by the power of his observation
> and the conscientious study of the facts of history;
> one should see also the philanthropist desirous
> of drawing from these laws practical consequences
> for the assistance of his fellow men. Everywhere,
> one feels his heart beating, and his love of human-
> ity forces from him at times concessions and com-
> promises and even contradictions with his prin-
> ciples."[46]

Woodrow Wilson, in his essay "An Old Master", speaks
of Smith's "large-hearted philosophy", of the "lumi-

nous, bracing work-a-day atmosphere that pervades his writings", of his "consummate style", and the "clear streams of practical wisdom and happy illustration which everywhere irrigate his expositions", and he also gives us this striking portrait:

> "Here, then is the picture of this Old Master: a quiet, awkward, forceful Scotsman, whose philosophy has entered everywhere into the life of politics and become a world force in thought; an impracticable Commissioner of Customs, who has left for the instruction of statesmen a theory of taxation; an unbusiness-like professor, who established the science of business; a man of books, who is universally honored by men of action; plain, eccentric, learned, inspired. The things that strike us most about him are his boldness of conception and the wideness of outlook, his breadth and comprehensiveness of treatment, and his carefully clarified and beautified style. He was no specialist, except *in the relations of things*."[47]

And finally we have the concluding words of a monograph by a successor of Smith's at the University of Glasgow and one of the most important of the recent students of his works, W. R. Scott:

> "His was in truth not only greatness, but a good greatness. All his influence was towards the broad and humane interpretation of the economic life, not as a pious aspiration, but worked out with the patience and the care of the scientist. Industry in investigation is fortunately not uncommon, but the power to gather up all the results and on the basis of these to enter into the future is very

precious, because it comes only at such very distant intervals. As one of the liberators of men's minds, Adam Smith has an acknowledged place amongst the remarkable intellects of the world, which is all his own, and which is confirmed to him in an increasing degree by the passing years."[48]

REFERENCES

[1] Becker, Carl L., "The Heavenly City of the Eighteenth Century Philosophers", New Haven, Yale University Press, 1932, p. 1.

[2] This is speaking broadly, for some are included whose lives just touched the 18th century.

[3] Becker, (op. cit.), pp. 33-4.

[4] Strong, G. B., "Adam Smith and the Eighteenth Century Concept of Social Progress", Chicago, University of Chicago Libraries, 1932, p. 8, quoting W. R. Inge in "Idea of Progress", p. 7.

[5] Scott, W. R., "Adam Smith", London, Oxford University Press, 1923, p. 4.

[6] "There were two chief tests of what was fixed in the apparent endless mutability of human affairs . . . The first of these — the element of common assent — was Cicero's 'ius naturale', which became prominent through the work of writers on Roman Law such as Grotius and Pufendorf. Thence it passed into the political writings of Locke and from him to France through Montesquieu and Voltaire. Natural Theology, too, had its effect in identifying the law of Nature with the law of God, and thus giving the former a religious sanction. From the idea of Nature in this sense came the conceptions of the light of Nature and a state of Nature." Ibid., pp. 4-5.

[7] Becker, (op. cit.), pp. 51-3, with quotation from Voltaire, "Oevres", XXV, p. 560.

[8] Of the general Chinese approach, especially in the realm of art, one penetrating student speaks of it as "the fusion of the rhythm of the spirit with the movement of living things." Binyon, Laurence, "The Flight of the Dragon", London, John Murray, 1911, p. 13; reprinted, 1927. Another writer tells of the interest of Leibnitz and Voltaire and later of Emerson in Chinese thought and civilization; and he asserts that the Physiocrats' "Natural Order" concept sprang largely from their study of Jesuit writings on China — their chief leader, Quesnay, being called by his followers "the Confucius of Europe". Bodde, Derk, "Chinese Ideas in the West", Washington, D.C., American Council on Education, 1948, pp. 15-23.

[9] Morrow, G. R., "The Ethical and Economic Theories of Adam

Smith", New York, Longmans, Green & Co., 1923, p. 12.

[10] Ibid.

[11] These thinkers are sometimes referred to as the "sentimental-ists" (See L. A. Selby-Bigge's "British Moralists", pp. vi and xxix-xx). Present connotations of the word make it inadequate as a title, but the original idea was sound — that which conveys the antithesis of extreme individualist rationalism. The development of this school of thought with its empirical viewpoint and strongly social conclu-sions is clearly set forth in a manuscript on "British Moral Philosophy after Hobbes, and the Ethics of Butler" by Prof. C. W. Hendel of Yale; it is available in the Yale Library.

[12] Morrow, (op. cit.), p. 26. A concise definition by Hume of sympathy as "that propensity we have to receive by communication (the) inclinations and sentiments of (others), however different from, or even contrary to, our own" is given by N. Kemp Smith in his "Philosophy of David Hume", p. 110.

[13] Becker, (op. cit.), pp. 102-3, including the four listed quota-tions that follow.

[14] Examination of the quoted Scriptural passages will of course indicate the omission of certain closely related ideas.

[15] Becker, (op. cit.), p. 39.

[16] See J. M. Clark in Clark, Douglas, et al., "Adam Smith, 1776-1926", Chicago, University of Chicago Press, 1928, pp. 57-65.

[17] Ibid., p. 57.

[18] Scott, W. R., "Adam Smith as Student and Professor", Glasgow, Jackson, Son & Co., 1937, p. 20.

[19] Ibid., p. 64.

[20] Rae, John, "Life of Adam Smith", London, The Macmillan Co., 1895, p. 1.

[21] Ibid., p. 9.

[22] Ibid., p. 12.

[23] Hirst, F. W., "Adam Smith", New York, The Macmillan Co., 1904, p. 7.

[24] Rae, (op. cit.), p. 12.

[25] Ibid., p. 178, first quotation, and p. 15, with reference to "Treatise". See Scott, (op. cit.), pp. 34-5 and 64, where the reli-ability of this story is now questioned; but whether it is true or not we know that within a few years Smith was becoming familiar with this and others of Hume's writings.

[26] Scott, (op. cit.), pp. 34 and 112-13.

[27] Rae, (op. cit.), p. 16.

[28] Smith, Adam, (op. cit.), ("The Wealth of Nations"), p. 718.

[29] Rae, (op. cit.), p. 24.

[30] Scott, (op. cit.), pp. 138-9.

[31] Rae, (op. cit.), pp. 54-5.

[32] Ibid., pp. 59-60.
[33] Ibid., pp. 141-4.
[34] Ibid., pp. 165 (pension) and 169 (successor); see Scott, (op. cit.), pp. 220-1, for records concerning Smith's resignation, in his faculty associates' estimate of him and his work.
[35] Becker, (op. cit.), p. 37.
[36] Rae, (op. cit.), pp. 196-7.
[37] Ibid., p. 284.
[38] Ibid., p. 405.
[39] See J. H. Hollander, in Clark, Douglas, Hollander, et al., "Adam Smith, 1776-1926" (op. cit.), pp. 23-4. The reference is to Buckle's "History of Civilization in England", Chapter IV, n. 60, or American Edition, I, 154-5.
[40] Rae, (op. cit.), p. 321.
[41] Ibid., p. 327.
[42] Ibid., pp. 409-11, and Scott, (op. cit.), pp. 228-30.
[43] Smith, Adam, "The Theory of Moral Sentiments", London, Henry G. Bohn, 1853, p. 176.
[44] Rae, (op. cit.), p. 430.
[45] Stewart, Dugald, "Account of the Life and Writings of Adam Smith, LL.D.", p. lxiv. This biographical sketch is bound with the "Theory" in the Bohn edition already referred to. See also Rae, (op. cit.), p. 434, for a fuller account of the burning of the manuscripts; see Scott, (op. cit.), pp. 57-8, for an account of how certain manuscripts escaped destruction and have but recently been rediscovered; see also Bullock, Charles J., "The Vanderblue Memorial Collection of Smithiana", Cambridge, Harvard University Press, 1939, p. ix.
[46] Delatour, Albert, "Adam Smith: Sa Vie, Ses Travaux, Ses Doctrines", Paris, Librairie Guillaumin et Cie., 1886. p. 314. (Translation by author of this study.)
[47] Wilson, Woodrow, "An Old Master and Other Political Essays", New York, Charles Scribner's Sons, 1893, pp. 10, 20, 22, and 25-26. R. B. Haldane, in his "Life of Adam Smith", London, Walter Scott, 1887, p. 57, makes this comment on Smith's style: "Had his ethical writings not assumed a systematic form, but been presented as a series of essays, written by an acute observer of men and things, upon the nature of certain human emotions, Adam Smith would, in all probability, have taken rank as one of the great essayists in English literature. The style is the simple, direct, eighteenth-century style which is the envy of those for whom it is a lost art".
[48] Scott, (op. cit.), ("Adam Smith"), p. 17.

CHAPTER THREE

SMITH'S SYSTEM OF THOUGHT — IN BRIEF

In dealing with Smith's thought one is confronted with the apparent contrast between the point of view of his two chief writings — a difficulty which has found its way into German social thought as "das Adam Smith — Problem". Attempts at solution have been made by differentiating the Smith of 1759 from the Smith of 1776, the change — from, seemingly, an idealistic to a materialistic point of view — being attributed chiefly to his contact, in the interim, with the Physiocrats in France.[1]

A. The Inter-relatedness of His Ideas

The writer is convinced, however, that this conflict is only a seeming one (though hardly less harmful in its historical effect than if genuine). This conclusion has been reached by a consideration of both internal and external evidence. The former — that is, the coherence of the ideas themselves — will be developed in the material that is to follow (in section B of this chapter). The latter has already been presented in essence in Chapter Two, but it may well be reviewed here. It is, first of all, the fact that Smith's lectures at Glasgow included both the ethical and the politico-economic ideas that were later developed, respectively, in the "Theory of Moral Sentiments" (hereafter, "Theory") and the "Inquiry into the Nature and Causes

of the Wealth of Nations" (hereafter, "Inquiry").
This is made clear by the outline given by his pupil
and later colleague, John Millar.[2] Also, the copy of
the student's notes on the last two sections of the lectures shows that most of the specific ideas later embodied in the "Inquiry" were being taught as part of
the general course at the time Smith was working on
his "Theory".[3]

A still more recent discovery of a manuscript described by Scott as an early draft of the "Inquiry",
made in 1935, adds yet further evidence of the earliness
— before the continental tour and his contact with the
Physiocrats — of the major ideas of the later work.
Scott writes in his preface:

> "Increasing knowledge of Adam Smith shows
> that the secret of his genius is to be found in that
> part of his life before he became celebrated,
> which may be conveniently dated as the period
> before he went to France . . ."[4]

Smith's contemporary and biographer, Stewart, says
positively, "Smith's political lectures, comprehending
the fundamental principles of his 'Inquiry' were delivered at Glasgow as early as the year 1752 or 1753."[5]

Rae quotes a paper which Smith read before the
Glasgow Economic Society in 1755 in which some of
the characteristic ideas and phrases of the "Inquiry"
appear and in which Smith definitely claims that these
ideas were included in his lectures in Edinburgh six
years previously and since then in his Glasgow lectures.[6]

Moreover, in the "Advertisement" for the 1790 revised edition of the "Theory", prepared by Smith just
before his death, he further indicated the connection

between his two main works in his own mind with the following words:

"In the last paragraph of the first edition of the present work, I said that I should in another discourse endeavour to give an account of the general principles of law and government, and of the different revolutions which they have undergone in the different ages and periods of society; not only in what concerns justice, but in what concerns police, revenue, and arms, and whatever else is the object of law. In the 'Inquiry concerning the Nature and Causes of the Wealth of Nations', I have partly executed this promise; at least so far as concerns police, revenue, and arms. What remains, the theory of jurisprudence, which I have long projected, I have hitherto been hindered from executing by the same occupations which had till now prevented me from revising the present work. Though my very advanced age leaves me, I acknowledge, very little expectation of ever being able to execute this great work to my own satisfaction; yet, as I have not altogether abandoned the design, and as I wish still to continue under the obligation of doing what I can, I have allowed the paragraph to remain as it was published more than thirty years ago, when I entertained no doubt of being able to execute everything which it announced."[7]

In reality, as we shall see in an examination of the ideas themselves, the economics work presupposes the ethical work published years earlier — a point well made by Woodrow Wilson in his essay already referred to, in which he says:

"It is interesting to note that even this vast miscellany of thought, the 'Wealth of Nations', systematized though it be, was not meant to stand alone as the exposition of a complete system; it was only a supplement to the 'Theory of Moral Sentiments'; and the two together constituted only chapters in that vast book of thought which their author would have written."[8]

With these "external" indications in mind of the over-all "togetherness" of Smith's ideas,[9] let us go on to the consideration of the main aspects of his thought, including the question of whether or not these aspects are in themselves inter-related.

B. Outline of His Thought — in His "Theory" and "Inquiry"

The choice of pattern for the arrangement of the relevant materials is an arbitrary one; but it has seemed well to the writer to seek to present this perforce brief survey in such a way that the answers will appear to three questions one naturally asks about creative theories: What is the goal that is sought, the concept of "what ought to be"? What is the analysis of our present situation, the understanding of "what is"? And what is the means put forward for resolving the tension between the two, that is, of moving toward the goal from where we are?

1. The General Aim

There are certain passages in both the "Theory" and the "Inquiry" which give quite definite indications of what Smith's ideas were of the goals to be sought. The aim of his efforts in the former is to find and

present the answers to the two questions which he
says are fundamental to the treatment of ethics:

> "First, wherein does virtue consist — or what is
> the tone of temper, and temper of conduct, which
> constitutes the excellent and praiseworthy char-
> acter, the character which is the natural object of
> esteem, honour, and approbation?
>
> "And, secondly, by what power or faculty in
> the mind is it that this character, whatever it be,
> is recommended to us? Or, in other words, how
> and by what means does it come to pass, that the
> mind prefers one tenor of conduct to another; de-
> nominates the one right and the other wrong;
> considers the one as the object of approbation,
> honour, and reward, and the other of blame, cen-
> sure, and punishment?"[10]

His precise answers to these questions will be dealt
with in the following sections, but we may well note
here, as basic, his association of perfection and happiness as human goals, as in the passage where he
says:

> "Nature . . . (in this situation) seems, as upon
> all other occasions, to have intended the happiness
> and perfection of the species."[11]

Elsewhere, too, we read of "the scheme which the
Author of Nature has established for the happiness
and perfection of the world".[12] It should be noted, too,
that this happiness is inclusive in character, not limited
to a few:

> "Man was made for action, and to promote by
> the exertion of his faculties such changes in the

external circumstances both of himself and others as may seem most favourable to the happiness of all."[13]

"All constitutions of government . . . are valued only in proportion as they tend to promote the happiness of those who live under them. This is their sole use and end."[14]

As a medial goal, with very important relation to the endeavor to secure happiness and perfection, we have the general social aim of "the harmony of society".[15] And as part of the foundation of harmony and concord there is the goal of "justice", a major part of which is "security from injury".[16]

Of the aims of political economy, Smith gives us this precise formulation in the "Inquiry":

> "Political economy, considered as a branch of the science of a statesman or legislator, proposes two distinct objects: first, to provide a plentiful revenue or subsistence for the people, or more properly to enable them to provide such a revenue or subsistence for themselves; and secondly, to supply the state or commonwealth with a revenue sufficient for the public services. It proposes to enrich both the people and the sovereign."[17]

As a medial goal in this area he sets up "perfect liberty", which, however, does not mean anarchy, as we shall see, since it is combined with justice, which involves law.[18]

And finally, with regard to the direction of economic activities, he says that "consumption is the sole end and purpose of all production" and that "the interest of the producer ought to be attended to only so far as it may be necessary for promoting that of the consumer".[19]

"Unless we use the produce of our industry, unless we subsist more people in a better way, what avails it?"[20]

Thus, in combined summary we have as the highest human goal the coupled aims of perfection and general happiness, which involves social harmony, which in turn involves justice, responsible liberty, and provision of the best obtainable standard of living for all people and sufficient revenue for the effective functioning of the state.

2. Analysis of the Individual and Society

In the "Theory" Smith speaks of "the present misery and depravity of the world" and, again, of "the present depraved state of mankind";[21] and in the "Inquiry" he gives examples of "savage injustice".[22] However, he believed there was hope of rectification, for "Nature does not seem to have dealt so unkindly with us as to have endowed us with any principle which is wholly and in every respect evil, or which, in no degree and in no direction, can be the proper object of praise and approbation."[23]

a. Man as Basically Social, with Justice of Central Significance

Examining some of these principles, we come first to the concept of man's social character — highly significant from a sociological standpoint (Smith has been spoken of as deserving "the first place among sociologists").[24] Man, we read, "can subsist only in society" and all society's members need one another's help.

This cooperation is most adequately founded on "love"; but it may be based on "utility"; and it can survive if injustice does not become characteristic.

"Where the necessary assistance is reciprocally afforded from love, from gratitude, from friendship, and esteem, the society flourishes and is happy. All the different members of it are bound together by the agreeable bands of love and affection, and are, as it were, drawn to one common centre of mutual good offices.

"But though the necessary assistance should not be afforded from such generous and disinterested motives, though among the different members of the society there should be no mutual love and affection, the society though less happy and agreeable, will not necessarily be dissolved. Society may subsist among different men, as among different merchants, from a sense of its utility, without any mutual love or affection; and though no man in it should owe any obligation, or be bound in gratitude to any other, it may still be upheld by a mercenary exchange of good offices according to an agreed valuation.

"Society, however, cannot subsist among those who are at all times ready to hurt and injure one another. The moment that injury begins, the moment that mutual resentment and animosity take place, all the bands of it are broken asunder, and the different members of which it consisted are, as it were, dissipated and scattered abroad by the violence and opposition of this discordant affections. If there is any society among robbers and murderers, they must at least, according to the trite observation, abstain from robbing and murdering one another. Beneficence, therefore, is less essential to the existence of society than justice. Society may subsist, though not in the most comfortable state, without beneficence; but the prevalence of injustice must utterly destroy it . . . Justice . . . is the main pillar that upholds the whole edifice."[25]

Another highly significant passage, presenting a challenge to the extreme individualism of some writers of the period, speaks of society as the "mirror" without which the individual could not come to full human stature:

"Were it possible that a human creature could grow up to manhood in some solitary place, without any communication with his own species, he could no more think of his own character, of the propriety or demerit of his own sentiments and conduct, of the beauty or deformity of his own mind, than of the beauty or deformity of his own face. All these are objects which he cannot easily see, which naturally he does not look at, and with regard to which he is provided with no mirror which can present them to his view.

"Bring him into society, and he is immediately provided with the mirror which he wanted before. It is placed in the countenance and behaviour of those he lives with, which always mark when they enter into, and when they disapprove of his sentiments; and it is here that he first views the propriety or impropriety of his own passions, the beauty and deformity of his own mind".[26]

Thus society is not regarded as merely a collection of individuals but as having a real character of its own and a function necessary for the development of persons. Perfect harmony, as we have seen, is a goal to be striven for, but there is an underlying partial harmony present without which society could not go on. The patient is sick but not unto death as long as there is a basic minimum of health, for, Smith writes:

> "If a nation could not prosper without the enjoyment of perfect liberty and perfect justice, there is not in the world a nation which could ever have prospered. In the political body, however, the wisdom of nature has fortunately made ample provision for remedying many of the bad effects of the folly and injustice of man; in the same manner as it has done in the natural body, for remedying those of his sloth and intemperance."[27]

This underlying principle of societal health expresses itself, we learn, as sympathy.

b. Sympathy, the Basic Principle of Society's Health

Smith's analysis of sympathy and the way it works is of genuine significance for an understanding of his whole approach. His briefest definition is based on etymology:

> "Sympathy . . . may . . . be made use of to denote our fellow-feeling with any passion whatever."[28]

It is that experience through which we come to understand another's feelings and actions as "by imagination we place ourselves in his situation". This fellow-feeling possibility applies both to the actor and the spectator — each seeking to put himself in the other's place and to act accordingly, in a two-way process by which understanding and concord may be reached or at least approximated.

"Society and conversation, therefore, are the most powerful remedies for restoring the mind to its tranquillity, if, at any time, it has unfortunately lost it; as well as the best preservatives of that equal and happy temper, which is so necessary to self-satisfaction and enjoyment."[29]

"Sympathy . . . enlivens joy and alleviates grief."[30]

Its relation to the phenomenon of approval is analyzed as follows:

"When we approve of any character or action, the sentiments we feel are . . . derived from four sources, which are in some respects different from one another. First, we sympathize with the motives of the agent; secondly we enter into the gratitude of those who receive the benefit of his actions; thirdly, we observe that his conduct has been agreeable to the general rules by which those two sympathies generally act; and, last of all, when we consider such actions, as making a part of a system of behaviour which tends to promote the happiness either of the individual or of the society, they appear to derive a beauty from this utility, not unlike that which we ascribe to any well-contrived machine."[31]

Disapproval could be analyzed in the same way — each factor being expressed negatively.

Smith escapes pure subjectivism and relativism in this interpretation of sympathy by his concept of *"the impartial and well-informed spectator"*, the "man within the breast" who is "the great judge and arbiter of conduct".[32]   The ultimate character and grounding of this interior spectator, or conscience, will be discussed in the following chapter, but the concept of its existence and authority should be noted in this connection, for "it is only by consulting this judge within that we can ever see what relates to ourselves in its proper shape and dimensions, or that we can ever make any proper comparison between our own interests and those of other people".[33] The *norm*, therefore — the higher court of appeal — is the viewpoint of this ideal impartial spectator, to which each of the parties concerned in any consideration endeavors, through the process of fellow-feeling, to make his own attitudes and actions conform.

It is along this line that Smith answers the second of the two questions he speaks of as basic to a treatment of ethics — that is, by what power or faculty the character of virtue commends itself to us.

c. What is Virtue?

Thus we come to the first question (the two being dealt with in this reverse order by Smith, also), as to what constitutes virtue.   His analyses of various historical attempts by both ancients and moderns to deal with and answer this question are among the very interesting parts of the "Theory", but a summary such as this is obviously not the place to discuss them.   His own answer is given clearly and succinctly:

> "The man who acts according to the rules of perfect prudence, of strict justice, and of proper benevolence, may be said to be perfectly virtuous."[34]

These aspects of complete virtue are important in themselves but even more so in their right relationship.

Prudence is the virtue which has as its proper business "the care of the health, of the fortune, of the rank and reputation of the individual, the objects upon which his comfort and happiness in this life are supposed principally to depend".[35] And the prudent man is characterized by sincerity, steady and faithful friendship, decency and inoffensiveness, industry, frugality, and contentment with "continuous though small" accumulations of fortune.[36] It is thus a respectable and "in some degree . . . an amiable and agreeable quality", but it certainly is not the most endearing or ennobling of virtues.

> "It commands a certain cold esteem, but seems not entitled to any very ardent love or admiration."[37]

It should be noted, too, that Smith elsewhere in effect extends this individual concept of prudence to include the care of the family, the welfare of the "great society of mankind" being furthered by "directing the principal attention of each individual to that particular portion of it" (society) which is "most within the sphere of his abilities and of his understanding".[38]

The chief object of *justice* is, as we have already noted, "the security from injury". And its "most sacred laws" are those "which guard the life and person of our neighbour" — and of course of his neighbors, including ourselves; "the next are those which guard his property and possessions; and last of all come those which guard what are called his personal rights, or what is due to him from the promises of others".[39] In one of his most vivid passages Smith shows how sympathy and justice are related:

"We must here, as in all other cases, view ourselves not so much according to that light in
which we naturally appear to ourselves, as according to that in which we naturally appear to others.
Though every man may, according to the proverb,
be the whole world to himself, to the rest of mankind he is a most insignificant part of it.   Though
his own happiness may be of more importance
to him than that of all the world besides, to every
other person it is of no more consequence than
that of any other man.

"Though it may be true, therefore, that every
individual, in his own breast, naturally prefers
himself to all mankind, yet he dares not look mankind in the face and avow that he acts according
to this principle.   He feels that in this preference
they can never go along with him, and that how
natural soever it may be to him, it must always
appear excessive and extravagant to them.   When
he views himself in the light in which he is conscious that others will view him, he sees that to
them he is but one of the multitudes, in no respect
better than any other in it.

"If he would act so as that the impartial spectator may enter into the principles of his conduct,
which is what of all things he has the greatest
desire to do, he must upon this, as upon all other
occasions, humble the arrogance of his self-love,
and bring it down to something which other men
can go along with . . . In the race for wealth, and
honours, and preferments, he may run as hard as
he can, and strain every nerve and every muscle,
in order to outstrip all competitors.   But if he
should justle, or throw down any of them, the

indulgence of the spectators is entirely at an end. It is a violation of fair play, which they cannot admit of. This man is to them, in every respect, as good as he; they do not enter into that self-love, by which he prefers himself so much to this other, and cannot go along with the motive from which he hurt him. They readily, therefore, sympathize with the natural resentment of the injured, and the offender becomes the object of their hatred and indignation. He is sensible that he becomes so, and feels that those sentiments are ready to burst out from all sides against him."[40]

Thus justice involves the spirit and practice of fair play and laws and proceedings designed to protect men against treatment of any kind that violates this fairness. As such it is "the foundation of civil government" — "the main pillar that upholds the whole edifice" of society.[41]

"The rules of justice," he writes, "may be compared to the rules of grammar; the rules of the other virtues to the rules which critics lay down for the attainment of what is sublime and elegant in composition." These rules he regards as founded on principles which are the subject of a special science, "of all sciences by far the most important, but hitherto, perhaps, the least cultivated — that of natural jurisprudence".[42]

Benevolence is made up of what Smith calls "the amiable and respectable virtues", such as humanity, love for others, sensibility, magnanimity, generosity, charity, "kindness or beneficence". These are the virtues which lead to the perfecting of men.

"And hence it is, that to feel much for others, and little for ourselves, that to restrain our selfish,

and to indulge our benevolent, affections, constitutes the perfection of human nature; and can
alone produce among mankind the harmony of
sentiments and passions in which consists their
whole grace and propriety. As to love our neighbour as we love ourselves is the great law of Christianity, so it is the great precept of nature to love
ourselves only as we love our neighbour, or, what
comes to the same thing, as our neighbour is
capable of loving us."[43]

These benevolent virtues are clearly superior to
those of prudence and justice — of "self-interest regu-
lated by justice" as one writer has phrased Smith's
approach, in part[44] — and they differ in that they are
beyond the sphere of social regulation. "Beneficence
is always free, it cannot be extorted by force." For
to oblige a man to perform an act of benevolence,
even if he ought clearly to carry it out, "would, if
possible, be still more improper than his neglecting to
perform it".[45] Injustice, however, is "the proper object of resentment and of punishment . . ." for:

"Upon this is founded that remarkable distinc-
tion between justice and all the other social
virtues . . . that we feel ourselves to be under
a stricter obligation to act according to justice,
than agreeably to friendship, charity, or generosity; that the practice of these last-mentioned
virtues seems to be left in some measure to our
own choice, but that, somehow or other, we feel
ourselves to be in a peculiar manner tied, bound,
and obliged, to the observation of justice. We
feel, that is to say, that force may, with the ut-
most propriety, and with the approbation of all

mankind, be made use of to constrain us to observe the rules of the one, but not to follow the precepts of the other."[46]

Carrying on his comparison of justice and benevolence, he writes that on the one hand while injustice deserves punishment, non-benevolence does not, and on the other while benevolent acts merit "the liveliest gratitude" and "highest reward", acts of justice, however important and necessary, deserve, and receive, no more than ordinary approbation.[47]

Benevolence broadens its scope until it is universal in character. We seldom, he says, are able to be effectively beneficent beyond the borders of our own country, but nevertheless "our good will is circumscribed by no boundary, but may embrace the immensity of the universe", and he continues:

"We cannot form the idea of any innocent and sensible being whose happiness we should not desire, or to whose misery, when distinctly brought home to our imagination, we should not have some degree of aversion."[48]

There follows an eloquent passage, which, though belonging most relevantly to the next chapter, it seems well to include here also:

"The idea of that divine Being, whose benevolence and wisdom have from all eternity contrived and conducted the immense machine of the universe so as at all times to produce the greatest possible quantity of happiness, is certainly, of all the objects of human contemplation by far the most sublime. Every other thought necessarily appears mean in comparison."[49]

After this flight to the infinite, Smith returns, characteristically, to what might be called "the business at hand" with the remark that after all "the administration of the great system of the universe . . . is the business of God, and not of man". Man's job is more humble and more fitted to his powers — "the care of his own happiness, of that of his family, his friends, his country"; and he should constantly remember that being "occupied in contemplating the more sublime can never be an excuse for his neglecting the more humble department"; that "the most sublime speculation of the contemplative philosopher can scarce compensate the neglect of the smallest active duty".[50]

It should constantly be borne in mind that however strong Smith's admiration for the benevolent virtues, he specifically parted company with his teacher Hutcheson and others who tend to make benevolence, by whatever name it is called, the sole constituent of true virtue. He agrees that there are various "not improbable arguments" advanced to persuade us that only benevolence may be ascribed to Deity, who needs nothing external to Himself. But, he says:

> ". . . Whatever may be the case with the Deity, so imperfect a creature as man, the support of whose existence requires so many things external to him, must often act from many other motives. The condition of human nature were peculiarly hard if those affections which, by the very nature of our being, ought frequently to influence our conduct, could, upon no occasion, appear virtuous, or deserve esteem and commendation from any body."[51]

Full virtue for man, then, is a combination of prudence, justice, and benevolence, but it is not merely the knowledge of these associated virtues which is emphasized but also their effective practice in all situations, through *self-command*. This is so stressed as to become almost a fourth component of true virtue, though it seems on the whole more accurate to regard it, in Smith's thought, as the effective carrying into action of the other three:

> "To act according to the dictates of prudence, of justice, and proper beneficence,[52] seems to have no great merit where there is no temptation to do otherwise. But *to act with cool deliberation* in the midst of the greatest dangers and difficulties; to observe religiously the sacred rules of justice, in spite both of the greatest interests which might tempt and the greatest injuries which might provoke us to violate them; never to suffer the benevolence of our temper to be damped or discouraged by the malignity and ingratitude of the individuals towards whom it may have been exercised, is the character of the most exalted wisdom and virtue. Self-command is not only itself a great virtue, but from it all the other virtues seem to derive their principal lustre."[53]

With such characteristics as its component parts, "virtue is excellence, something uncommonly great and beautiful, which rises far above what is vulgar and ordinary".[54] One who achieves even an approximation of such qualities will have "the great characteristics of virtue" — to deserve love and to deserve reward" — and through the sympathetic response of his fellows will achieve a large degree of the goal of

happiness; for "What so great happiness as to be beloved, and to know that we deserve to be beloved?
What so great misery as to be hated, and to know we
deserve to be hated?"[55]

As we move from prudence to justice to benevolence
we see that each step or level represents a higher stage
of consciousness of one's membership in society and
of the obligations and opportunities that membership
implies in the exercise of wider and deeper sympathy;
but no one supplants another, all remaining as vital
complementary parts of the good life.[56]

d. What is Real Wealth?

This brings us to Smith's area of concern in "The
Wealth of Nations" which is both obviously and
confessedly (by the very title of the work) in the
sphere of societal prudence, with its concern, among
other things, with the care of fortune or wealth. There
is some treatment, too, of justice, as a restraining force
on self-interest; but the sphere of benevolence is not
even approached, either in fact or in design. There
is indeed a very large number of subjects considered,
as even a quick glance at the table of contents will
reveal, but they are dealt with from the standpoint of
material well-being — one aspect of Smith's thought
which, we recall, he had hoped to bring into a com-
posite whole, "une veritable 'Histoire de la Civilisation' ".[57]

The first question of the two that are implicit in the
title of the "Inquiry" is of course, "What is the nature
of a nation's wealth?" And the most concise answer
he gives is in the last sentence of his introduction,
where he speaks of "the real wealth" as "the annual
produce of the land and labour of society".[58] This,

as the editor points out, should be read in conjunction with the first two paragraphs, when it then becomes clear "that the wealth of a nation is to be reckoned by its per capita income" or, in other words, its per capita share of the produce. The opening two paragraphs themselves are:

> "The annual labour of every nation is the fund which originally supplies it with all the necessaries and conveniences of life which it annually consumes, and which consist always either in the immediate produce of that labour, or in what is purchased with that produce from other nations.
> "According, therefore, as this produce or what is purchased with it, bears a greater or smaller proportion to the number of those who are to consume it, the nation will be better or worse supplied with all the necessaries and conveniences for which it has occasion."[59]

This view is in sharp contrast with the prevailing mercantilist doctrine of the time — against which Smith tilts throughout the work, that "the quantity of the precious metals which circulate" in a country constitutes the real wealth.[60]

Money, Smith asserts, is "the great wheel or circulation, the great instrument of commerce", and as such it is indeed important, but it "makes no part of the revenue of the society to which it belongs".[61]

e. What are the Causes of Wealth?

The second question implicit in the title — "What are the causes of a nation's wealth, the real forces which produce and increase it?" — has been partially answered in the above quotation. The sources are land and labor. Smith was the first of modern economists to enunciate clearly the famous "labor theory of value", destined to be further developed by Ricardo and then to be used by Marx and Engels as a basis for their economic theory of revolution. Perhaps its clearest formulation is that which appears in Chapter V, where we read:

> "At all times and places that is dear which it is difficult to come at, or which it costs much labour to acquire; and that cheap which is to be had easily, or with very little labour. Labour alone, therefore, never varying in its own value, is alone the ultimate and real standard by which the value of all commodities can at all times and places be estimated and compared. It is their real price; money is their nominal price only."[62]

The "natural recompense or wages of labour" is what it produces, and originally it all belonged to the laborer.

> "In that original state of things which precedes both the appropriation of land and the accumulation of stock, the whole produce of labour belongs to the labourer. He has neither landlord or master to share with him.
> "Had this state continued, the wages of labour would have augmented with all those improvements in its productive powers, to which the division of labour gives occasion."[63]

f. The Three Main Divisions of Income

The situation was changed, however, when land was appropriated and stock was accumulated. "As soon as land becomes private property the landlord demands a share of almost all the produce which the labourer can either raise or collect from it"[64] — his rent making the first deduction from what originally belonged entirely to the laborer who worked on the land.

The second deduction is the profit demanded for the use of stock by those who have accumulated it, whether the work be on the land or in the workshop. The amount each party gets depends on bargaining between them, especially between the owners of stock and laborers, and the former almost always has the advantage:

> "What are the common wages of labour, depends everywhere upon the contract usually made between these two parties, whose interests are by no means the same. The workmen desire to get as much, the masters to give as little as possible. The former are disposed to combine in order to raise, the latter in order to lower the wages of labour.
>
> "It is not, however, difficult to foresee which of the two parties must, upon all ordinary occasions, have the advantage in the dispute, and force the other into a compliance with their terms. The masters, being fewer in number, can combine much more easily, and the law, besides, authorizes, or at least does not prohibit, their combinations, while it prohibits those of the workmen. We have no acts of parliament against combining to lower the price of work, but many against combining to raise it. In all such disputes, the masters can hold out much longer . . . In the long run, the workman may be as necessary to his master as his master is to him, but the necessity is not so immediate."[65]

Thus the produce of the land is divided into the three categories of rents, wages, and profits — the income of three separate "orders of people" who have existed since the beginning of "civilized society".[66]

g. *The Division of Labor*

Smith was fascinated by the division of labor and wrote most interestingly, and often eloquently, of its effects. The great increase in quantity of output as a result of the division he analyzes as being due to the improvement of the dexterity of the workmen (resulting from specialization), the saving of time (consumed in shifting from one operation to another), and the application of proper machinery (the invention of which is speeded up by the simplification of functions with resulting concentration). His example of the results of this process in pin-making is famous, as is the closing paragraph of the first chapter of the "Inquiry" in which he pictures most vividly the complex economic inter-relatedness of his contemporary society:

"To say nothing of such complicated machines as the ship of the sailor, the mill of the fuller, or even the loom of the weaver, let us consider only what a variety of labour is requisite in order to form that very simple machine, the shears with which the shepherd clips the wool. The miner, the builder of the furnace for smelting the ore, the feller of the timber, the burner of the charcoal to be made use of in the smelting-house, the brick-maker, the brick-layer, the workmen who attend the furnace, the mill-wright, the forger, the smith, must all of them join their different arts in order to produce them . . . If we examine, I say, all these things, and consider what a variety of labour is employed about each of them, we shall be sensible that without the assistance and cooperation of many thousands, the very meanest person in a civilized country could not be provided, even according to, what we very falsely imagine, the easy and simple manner in which he is commonly accomodated."[67]

(What would Smith say could he inspect a twentieth century automaton?)

h. The Underlying Motive

How is this remarkable cooperation brought about and maintained? We already have Smith's answer implicitly in the definition of prudence as the virtue whose proper business is "the care of the health, of the fortune, of the rank and reputation of the individual".[68] It is the interest in the self's maximum well-being, "the desire of bettering our condition . . . which . . . comes with us from the womb and never leaves us till we go into the grave"; and he asserts that most men try to better their condition by "the most vulgar and the most obvious" means, that of augmenting their fortune.[69]

This force, "the natural effort of every individual to better his own condition" is, he maintains, so powerful as to be able by itself to carry on the society to wealth and prosperity.[70] This is entirely, we recall, within the sphere of prudence, and Smith argues that in this material realm in which "man has almost constant occasion for the help of his brethren", it is vain for him to expect it from their benevolence only. "He will be more likely to prevail if he can interest their self-love in his favour, and show them that it is for their own advantage to do for him what he requires of them."[71]

This self-interest, plus what Smith speaks of as "a certain propensity in human nature . . . to truck, barter, and exchange one thing for another",[72] is the basic motive underlying the vast interdependent economic organization. Not only does Smith regard "the consideration of his own private profit" as "the sole motive" directing the activities of "the owner of capital", but he speaks of profit as "of all encouragements the greatest and most effectual", and he expresses suspicion of those "who affect to trade for the public good" ("an affectation, indeed, not very common among merchants").[73] And he maintains that if there is no interference, the quantity of production will regulate itself in accordance with the effectual demand, "or according to the demand of those who are willing to pay the whole rent, labour and profits which must be paid in order to prepare and bring it (the produce) to market".[74]

i. The "Invisible Hand"

Above all is the guiding force of "an invisible hand" which keeps the various individual activities so integrated as to further the welfare of the whole society, even though the individuals are only conscious of working for their own ends;[75] what might be called the spiritual orientation of this force will be dealt with in the next chapter.

It would be quite false, however, to consider Smith as satisfied with the "status quo". No, mankind was in "a depraved state" which included "savage injustices", as we have seen.[76]

j. Evils to be Combatted

The greatest evil in the political-economic realm he considered to be *the mercantile system* which, with its false presuppositions on the nature of wealth and various devices such as export bounties and prohibitive tariffs and the like, he attacked with all the vigor of a knight in combat.

An allied evil, in Smith's thought, is that of *monopolies of all kinds* — including those in the educational and ecclesiastical realms — which he thoroughly disliked and fought with every weapon in his command, including some very telling sarcasm. In his day, the clearest examples were the East India Companies — both British and Dutch — and of them he writes:

> "Such exclusive companies . . . are nuisances in every respect; always more or less inconvenient to the countries in which they are established, and destructive to those which have the misfortune to fall under their government."[77]

But it was the monopolizing spirit as such to which he was most basically opposed, identifying it as "mean rapacity":

> "The violence and injustice of the rulers of mankind is an ancient evil, for which, I am afraid, the nature of human affairs can scarce admit of a remedy. But the mean rapacity, the monopolizing spirit of merchants and manufacturers, who neither are, nor ought to be, the rulers of mankind, though it cannot perhaps be corrected, may very easily be prevented from disturbing the tranquillity of anybody but themselves."[78]

These monopolistic interests have organized themselves to protect their privileges against "us", the
public; in fact, "conspiracy against the public" on their
part is almost a daily occurrence, and must not be
ignored or encouraged:

> "People of the same trade seldom meet together,
> even for merriment and diversion but the conversa-
> tion ends in a conspiracy against the public, or in
> some contrivance to raise prices. It is impossible
> indeed to prevent such meetings, by any law
> which either could be executed, or would be con-
> sistent with liberty and justice. But though the
> law cannot hinder people of the same trade from
> sometimes assembling together, it ought to do
> nothing to facilitate such assemblies; much less
> to render them necessary."[79]

Moreover, he maintained, this effort to raise prices
was "by no means for the benefit of the workman" but
because of "the avidity of our great manufacturers";
and all this he found to be aided and abetted by the
mercantile system which favored "the industry which
is carried on for the benefit of the rich and powerful".[80]
And their special privileges have been supported by
the passing of sometimes cruel laws — for example:

> "By the 8th of Elizabeth, Chapter Three, the
> exporter of sheep, lambs or rams was for the first
> offence to forfeit all his goods forever, to suffer
> a year's imprisonment, and then to have his left
> hand cut off in a market town upon a market day,
> to be there nailed up; and for the second offence
> to be adjudged a felon, and to suffer death accord-
> ingly."[81]

Such laws "which the clamour of our merchants and manufacturers has extorted from the legislature, for the support of their own absurd and oppressive monopolies" are "like the laws of Draco . . . written in blood".[82]

All such monopolistic forces are harmful to society, according to Smith — diseases of the body politic.

"It is thus that every system which endeavours, either by extraordinary encouragements, to draw towards a particular species of industry a greater share of the capital of the society than what would naturally go to it; or, by extraordinary restraints, to force from a particular species of industry some share of the capital which would otherwise be employed in it; is in reality subversive of the great purpose which it means to promote. It retards, instead of accelerating, the progress of the society towards real wealth and greatness; and diminishes, instead of increasing, the real value of the annual produce of its land and labour."[83]

3. The Process for Realizing the Goal

How, then, can "what is" be transformed so as to correspond more closely to "what ought to be" — the goals, for Smith, of perfection and general happiness as the ultimates, with harmony and justice, responsible freedom and material well-being as the medial aims?

a. In the "Theory"

The general methodology advocated for life as a whole has already been set forth in principle, being that of *imaginative sympathy*, mutual endeavor to put oneself into others' circumstances, which should lead to more effective cooperation.[84] And together with this there should be right-proportioned concern for the *three parts of full virtue* — concern for one's own and his family's well-being leading to the virtue of *prudence,* concern for fair-play leading to the virtue of *justice,* and concern for the happiness of others leading to the virtue of *benevolence* (or beneficence), *all made effective in action through self-command.*[85]

b. In the "Inquiry"

The methods suited to the promotion of the material well-being of society are *prudence, with freedom in justice, and specific government action as needed.*

For the increase of wealth free competition within the limits set by justice is advocated — the natural desire to better one's condition being not only given free play but stimulated as much as possible. The general maxim is:

> "In general, if any branch or trade, or any division of labour, be advantageous to the public, the freer and more general the competition, it will always be the more so."

This means, in the first place, the "moderate and gradual relaxation"[87] of the laws that favor monopolistic industries, in the direction of free competition; however, their complete removal would be desirable and would have fine results:

> "All systems either of preference or of restraint, therefore, being thus completely taken away, the obvious system of natural liberty establishes itself of its own accord. Every man, as long as he does not violate the laws of justice, is left perfectly free

to pursue his own interest his own way, and to bring both his industry and capital into competition with those of any other man, or order of men."[88]

However, he thinks it Utopian to expect that freedom of trade could ever be completely restored in Great Britain, because of "the prejudices of the public" and "the private interests of many individuals";[89] but he strongly advocates moving as far as possible in that direction.

He maintains, as we have seen, that the interests of the consumers should always be recognized as paramount, with consumption as "the sole end and purpose of all production".[90] This certainly has not been recognized, he repeatedly shows — the whole mercantile system with its monopolies and imperialism having been carried on for the benefit of certain large-scale producers at the expense of smaller producers and the general public.[91]

As for *specific government action* he defines three areas in which this is needed:

(1) ". . . first, the duty of protecting the society from the violence and invasion of other independent societies;

(2) "secondly, the duty of protecting, as far as possible, every member of the society from the injustice or oppression of every other member of it, or the duty of establishing an exact administration of justice;

(3) "and thirdly, the duty of erecting and maintaining certain public works and certain public institutions."[92]

The first of these involves, of course, the military establishment, with regard to which Smith favors maintaining a standing army instead of the alternative of enforcing military service; this, he maintains, history demonstrates to be superior, especially in a more advanced stage of social development.[93]

The second area involves, as indicated, primarily legal activity carried out for the protection of all members of society. With reference to economic affairs in this connection he argues for laws favorable to workers. "Masters are always and everywhere," he says, "in a sort of tacit, but constant and uniform combination not to raise wages of labour above their actual rate . . . and sometimes enter into particular combinations to sink the wages of labour even below this rate;" and they already exercise so much influence in this direction as counselors of government that "when the regulation . . . is in favor of the workmen it is always just and equitable".[94] One well-known economic historian is so impressed with this tendency on Smith's part that he says that "when it comes to choosing between capitalists and workmen . . . it is quite clear . . . that Smith's sympathy was wholly with the workers"[95] — a judgment which many passages seem to validate. For example, in his chapter on "Wages of Labour", he writes:

"What improves the circumstances of the greater part can never be regarded as an inconveniency to the whole . . . It is but equity, besides, that they who feed, clothe and lodge the whole body of the people, should have such a share of the produce of their own labour as to be themselves tolerably well fed, clothed and lodged."[96]

Moreover, he argues, high wages are an encouragement to industry:

"The wages of labour are the encouragement of industry, which, like every other human quality improves in proportion to the encouragement it receives . . . Where wages are high, accordingly, we shall always find the workmen more active, diligent, and expeditious, than where they are low . . ."[97]

And, in contrast, we read:

"Our merchants and master-manufacturers complain much of the bad effects of high wages in raising the price, and thereby lessening the sale of their goods both at home and abroad. They say nothing concerning the bad effects of high profits."[98]

And he repeatedly expressed his strong opposition to slavery.[99]

Smith, indeed, was very much a democrat in basic principles. He was quite capable of rebuking "impertinence and presumption . . . in kings and ministers"[100] as well as their extravagance. And elsewhere he writes:

"The difference between the most dissimilar characters, between a philosopher and a common street porter, for example, seems to arise not so much from nature, as from habit, custom, and education."[101]

The third of the spheres in which he favors government action involves the building and maintenance of roads, the state management of the post-office, the legal limitation of interest rates, and the incorporation of such public utility enterprises as banking, insurance, canals, and waterworks.[102] It also includes elementary education at public expense,[103] an obligation not generally recognized at the time. He felt this was especially important because of the dulling effect of constantly performing very simple operations, due to the division of labor, which should be offset as much as possible for the sake of the individuals themselves and of the society of which they are members; his paragraph describing these harmful effects is penetrating and it leads to his conclusion that "this is the state into which the labouring poor, that is, the great body of the people, must necessarily fall, unless government takes some pains to prevent it".[104]

Also dealt with in this connection are the "institutions for the instruction of people of all ages", which are chiefly religious; he is opposed to legal establishment of a church, but he favors certain educational requirements for ministers as well as for other members of the liberal professions.[105]

The criterion for judging what should be supported by government is stated clearly in the following paragraph:

> "When the institutions or public works which are beneficial to the whole society, either cannot be maintained altogether, or are not maintained altogether by the contribution of such particular members of the society as are most immediately benefited by them, the deficiency must in most cases be made up by the general contribution of the whole society. The general revenue of the society, over and above defraying the expense of defending the society, and of supporting the dignity

of the chief magistrate, must make up for the deficiency of many particular branches of revenue."[106]

To obtain the necessary revenues he lays down the well-known internal taxation maxims for all citizens of:

— equality, meaning "in proportion to the revenue which they respectively enjoy under the protection of the state";
— certainty, meaning clearly known rather than arbitrary amounts;
— convenience of payment;
— economy of collection.[107]

As for tariffs, he favors the removal of all that are prohibitive in character, and, instead, "subjecting all foreign manufactures to such moderate taxes, as it was found from experience afforded upon each article the greatest revenue to the public" — "taxation being always employed as an instrument of revenue and never of monopoly".[108]

In summary, it would seem well to remind ourselves of the basic inter-relatedness of Smith's thought (as emphasized in the first part of this chapter) — a fact easy to lose sight of, due to what might be termed his academic habit of compartmentalizing his ideas. The "Theory" and the "Inquiry", we recall, are the published forms of only parts of his over-all approach made in his lectures in Moral Philosophy. That inter-relationship has been aptly expressed by a modern sociologist as follows:

"As the life-problem of individuals and nations presented itself to Adam Smith's mind, it was . . . first, a problem of religion; second, a problem of ethics; third, a problem of civil justice; fourth, a problem of economic technique."[109]

Having given some attention to the last three of these areas let us turn to a consideration of the first.

REFERENCES

[1] See Morrow, (op. cit.), pp. 4-9; Small, Albion W., "Adam Smith and Modern Sociology", Chicago, University of Chicago Press, 1907, p. 60; and Zeyss, "Adam Smith und der Eigennutz", Tübingen, Verlag der H. Lauup'schen Buchhandlung, 1889, p. 19, for a further discussion of this theory of a change in Smith.

[2] See Chapter Two, Section B. 2., and Rae, (op. cit.), pp. 54-5.

[3] See Chapter Two, Section B. 2., and Cannan, Edwin, "Lectures of Adam Smith", Oxford, Clarendon Press, 1896, Introduction.

[4] Scott, "Adam Smith as Student and Professor" (op. cit.), p. viii.

[5] Stewart in Smith, "The Theory of the Moral Sentiments" (op. cit.), p. lix.

[6] Rae, (op. cit.), pp. 62-3; see also Scott, (op. cit.), pp. 53-4 and 111.

[7] Smith, "The Works of Adam Smith", London, T. Cadell and W. Davies, 1812, Volume 1, pp. xiv-xv.

[8] Wilson, (op. cit.), pp. 16-17; see also Buckle, Henry Thomas, "History of Civilization in England", New York, D. Appleton and Company, 1858, Volume II, pp. 348-9; and Bagehot, Walter, "Economic Studies", London, Longmans, Green, & Co., 1880, pp. 133-4.

[9] Says James Bonar of Smith, "His constant effort is to relate parts to the whole, and the whole is as large as he can make it. This was a point of contact with philosophy; it was also the secret of much of his influence on economic study itself." "The Tables Turned", London, P. S. King & Son, Ltd., 1926, p. 10.

[10] "Theory" (op. cit.), pp. 391-2.

[11] Ibid., p. 152.

[12] Ibid., p. 235. It is interesting to note, too, that in the "Wealth of Nations" he quotes with approval as "the object which the ancient moral philosophy proposed to investigate", "the happiness and perfection of a man, considered not only as an individual, but as the member of a family, of a state, and of the great society of mankind". (op. cit.), p. 726.

[13] Ibid., pp. 153-4.

[14] Ibid., p. 266.

[15] Ibid., p. 23.

[16] "Lectures" (Cannan, ed., op. cit.), p. 3. See also "Theory" (op. cit.), p. 121.

[17] "Inquiry" (op. cit.), p. 397.

[18] Ibid., p. 572.

[19] Ibid., p. 625.

[20] "Lectures" (op. cit.), p. 205.

[21] "Theory" (op. cit.), pp. 63 and 109.

[22] "Inquiry" (op. cit.), p. 416.

[23] "Theory" (op. cit.), p. 109.

[24] Barnes, E. E. and Becker, Howard, "Social Thought from Lore to Science", New York, D. C. Heath and Co., 1938, p. 537 (quoting Giddings).

[25] "Theory" (op. cit.), pp. 124-5.

[26] Ibid., p. 162. See also Charles H. Cooley's thought of society as a mirror; Barnes and Becker, (op. cit.), Volume 1, pp. 928-30 and 984-5.

[27] "Inquiry" (op. cit.), p. 638.

[28] "Theory" (op. cit.), p. 5.

[29] Ibid., pp. 4, 22-3, 23-4, and 25.

[30] Ibid., p. 11.

[31] Ibid., pp. 479-80.

[32] Ibid., p. 185.

[33] Ibid., p. 191.

[34] Ibid., p. 349.

[35] Ibid., p. 311.

[36] Ibid., pp. 311-14.

[37] Ibid., pp. 315-16.

[38] Ibid., p. 337.

[39] Ibid., p. 121.

[40] Ibid., pp. 119-21, from a chapter entitled "Of a Sense of Justice . . ."

[41] Ibid., pp. 3 and 125; latter referred to earlier in footnote #25.

[42] Ibid., pp. 250 and 319.

[43] Ibid., pp. 26-38, 113-15, 52, and 27-8.

[44] Morrow, (op. cit.), p. 48.

[45] "Theory" (op. cit.), pp. 112 and 113.

[46] Ibid., p. 114.

[47] Ibid., p. 117.

[48] Ibid., p. 345.

[49] Ibid., p. 347.

[50] Ibid., p. 348.

[51] Ibid., pp. 440-7 and 446-7.

[52] "Beneficence" is used interchangeably with "benevolence" by Smith.

[53] "Theory" (op. cit.), p. 354.

[54] Ibid., p. 28.

[55] Ibid., p. 165.

[56] This inter-relatedness is stressed effectively by G. R. Morrow, (op. cit.), p. 57., when he says: "It is not adequate, therefore, to represent the higher virtues as the passage from egoism to altruism. The inferior virtues, i.e., self-interest restrained by justice, are in a very great degree social, for upon the free play of individual interests depends the material welfare of society . . . Nor do the higher virtues exclude self-interest; the perfectly virtuous man must preserve his own welfare, but he does it conscious of the relation of his own welfare to the good of the whole . . . The lower and the higher virtues are not opposed to one another, but are thoroughly in accord; they represent different levels of the social consciousness."

[57] Delatour, (op. cit.), pp. 76 and 314; see also Zeyss, (op. cit.), p. 19 (quoting Bagehot).

[58] "Inquiry" (op. cit.), p. lx.

[59] Ibid., p. lvii.

[60] Ibid., p. 324.

[61] Ibid., p. 276.

[62] Ibid., p. 33.

[63] Ibid., p. 64.

[64] Ibid., p. 65.

[65] Ibid., p. 66.

[66] Ibid., p. 248.

[67] Ibid., pp. 4-5, and 11-12.

[68] "Theory" (op. cit.), p. 311; also see above, Section 2. c.

[69] "Inquiry" (op. cit.), pp. 324 and 325.

[70] Ibid., p. 508.

[71] Ibid., p. 14.

[72] Ibid., p. 13.

[73] Ibid., pp. 355, 716, and 423.

[74] Ibid., p. 404.

[75] Ibid., p. 423.

[76] "Theory" (op. cit.), p. 109 and "The Wealth of Nations" (op. cit.), p. 416; and Section 2, before a.

[77] "Inquiry" (op. cit.), p. 606.

[78] Ibid., p. 460.

[79] Ibid., p. 438 and 128.

[80] Ibid., pp. 608-9.

[81] Ibid., p. 612.

[82] Ibid.

[83] Ibid., pp. 650-51. Speaking of such monopoly, he also writes, "To promote the little interest of one little order of mean in one country, it hurts the interest of all other orders of men in that country, and of all men in all other countries." Ibid., p. 578.

[84] "Theory" (op. cit.), pp. 23 and 124-5; see above Section 2. b.

[85] See above Section 2. c.

[86] "Inquiry" (op. cit.), p. 313.

[87] Ibid., p. 571.

[88] Ibid., p. 651.

[89] Ibid., pp. 437-8.

[90] Ibid., p. 625.

[91] Ibid., p. 626.

[92] Ibid., p. 651; paragraphing has been added.

[93] Ibid., pp. 653-60. (Treatment so brief because matter so technical.)

[94] "Theory" (op. cit.), p. 121 and "The Wealth of Nations" (op. cit.), pp. 66-7 and 142.

[95] Gide, Charles, and Rist, Charles, "A History of Economic Doctrines", New York, D. C. Heath and Co., 1915, p. 66.

[96] "Inquiry" (op. cit.), pp. 78-9.

[97] Ibid., p. 81.

[98] Ibid., p. 98.

[99] Ibid., pp. 80 and 365-6.

[100] Ibid., p. 329.

[101] Ibid., p. 15.

[102] Ibid., pp. 683 and 715.

[103] Ibid., pp. 735-8.

[104] Ibid., pp. 734-5.

[105] Ibid., pp. 740-66.

[106] Ibid., p. 768.

[107] Ibid., pp. 769-900, especially pp. 777-8.

[108] Ibid., pp. 834 and 836.

[109] Small, (op. cit.), (see footnote #1 above), p. 9.

CHAPTER FOUR

SMITH AND CHRISTIANITY

Before considering Smith's relationship to Christianity it seems well to indicate the meaning, as here understood, of two key concepts.

A. "Religion" and "Christianity"

1. Religion

"Religion" is here thought of as inclusive of both "faith" and "ethics", with the former made up of "theology" and "worship". Such a statement obviously calls for further effort at defining, as these terms are certainly not used in identical fashion by all; what follows may at least serve as a hypothesis for use in this study.

a. With respect first to the aspects of *faith*, may we think of *theology* as the disciplined intellectual endeavor to deal with the basic philosophic questions as to the implications of meaning in the cosmos — in nature and in human life — in the light of both reason and the fullest accepted revelation of God's nature and will?   Such an approach obviously stresses the closeness of theology and philosophy.   In fact, their tasks are thought of as identical in the formulation of the fundamental questions, their difference appearing in their methods of seeking answers to these questions. Philosophy is by its own choice limited to the use of reason alone.   Theology frankly supplements reason with revelation — whether embodied in the Old Testament or in the Bible as a whole and whether interpreted by Roman Catholics, Eastern Orthodox, or Protestants. This range of "accepted revelation" could be extended still further, of course, to include as possible sources the Qur'an of the Muslims or the sacred writings of Hindus, Buddhists, Taoists, or adherents of other religious groups; but for the purpose of this study we confine our attention to the historic Judeo-Christian religious heritage.

The assumption that there is "meaning" in life signifies the assurance that it is not merely "an accidental collocation of atoms"[1] — that, however hidden and misunderstood, there is a basic coherence and purpose which can be glimpsed and conformed to. Religions vary as to just *what* this meaning is but they all agree *that* it is.

May we think of *worship* as all that is involved in man's effort, individually and socially, to respond to the "meaning" he affirms — particularly to what he believes to be the will of what we may call "the center of meaning"? The various religions call this "center of meaning" by different names — "God", "Yahweh", "Allah", "Ahura Mazda", "Shang-Ti", etc. — but all agree that man must seek to respond to this central Being. The prophet Isaiah's experience in the Temple comes as close, probably, as is possible to the setting forth of the essential elements of true worship — vision and adoration, awareness and confession of sin, a sense of being forgiven and cleansed, a sense of being called to a task, acceptance of the call and commitment of the self, and the Divine commission.[2]

b. *Ethics* has already been defined for purposes of

this study in Chapter One,[3] but a repetition here, where it may be seen in context, may well be of some value. It is understood here, then, as the disciplined effort of mind and will to formulate and carry out what are believed to be the implications for human relations of either reason alone (philosophic ethics) or of reason and accepted revelation (theological ethics). Obviously this, in the latter form, has the closest relationship to both theology and worship and might even be considered as included in them, part in the one and part in the other. However, it is of such importance, especially in the Judeo-Christian approach to life, that it deserves individual emphasis as being virtually the equal of "faith" in significance — the two giving us, as has often been suggested, the "vertical" and the "horizontal" dimensions of life as religiously understood.

2. *Christianity*

What, then, is understood as the essence of that particular form of religion known as Christianity? Obviously, all that can be attempted in this brief section is to mention the core ideas which would be agreed to by large numbers of Christians, though each would doubtless want to add a good deal. Some confidence seems justified as to the essential character of these concepts, as they are based on a statement of the Christian faith set forth at one of the most widely representative (both denominationally and geographically) conferences of Christians in modern times, that which met near Madras, India, in 1939. The statement is included in full in Appendix #1 and all quotations not otherwise identified in the following summary come from it:

1. The concept of God as the "Holy Will" who is both world-creator — with all creation as essentially good[4] — and world-sustainer, with concern for order and "structure" and for "fidelity" and righteousness;

2. The concept of man as both "child of God", with unlimited potentiality for good, and also as alienated or estranged doer of evil, as sinner — the choice between good and evil being possible "in the mystery of the freedom which God has given him";

3. The concept of the historic Christ as the special revelation of God's nature and will and of what man ought to be — the Divine "Word"[5] incarnate in human existence — his life, suffering and death, and resurrection being together the clearest manifestation of "the victory of holiness and love over death and corruption" and thus laying the foundation for belief in the on-going life;

4. The concept of the Kingdom of God as in part a present reality and in part a future potentiality — to be "consummated in the final establishment of His glorious reign of Love and Righteousness";

5. The concept of the Holy Spirit — the "Spirit of Truth" in John's terminology[6] — as continually at work in the world;

6. The concept of the Church as a fellowship of disciples meant "to continue Christ's saving work in the world";

7. The concept of responsibility for all men — involving opposition to all injustice and support for efforts to secure the fullest spiritual and bodily health.

Taken in their entirety these ideas are the vital components of the fundamental Biblical concept of the "Covenant" (the real meaning of "Testament", of course, as used for the two parts of the Bible) as the Divine plan for the relationship of God and man, and of man and man.

In reality, it would be more accurate to speak of these concepts and the historical movements stemming from them as the "Judeo-Hellenic-Christian heritage" — thus stressing the generally recognized influence on the early Church of not only Judaism (especially the work of Moses and the great Prophets from Amos to Second Isaiah) but also that of the main Greek religio-philosophic tradition (especially as set forth in some of the thought of Socrates, Plato, Aristotle, and the Stoics). However, for the sake of simplicity we may use the word "Christianity", remembering the important background influences.

It should be added that this heritage forms the core of the presuppositions underlying this study, it seeming both honest and wise to acknowledge that fact explicitly. In the words of Karl Mannheim, with reference to a different area of concern, but relevant here:

> "A clear and explicit avowal of the implicit metaphysical presuppositions which underlie and make possible empirical knowledge will do more for the clarification and advancement of research than a verbal denial of the existence of these pre-suppositions accompanied by their surreptitious admission through the back door."[7]

Whether these assumptions are true or not is a problem whose solution lies beyond the scope of this book.

B. Smith's Relationship to Christianity — Explicitly

1. In Life

As already pointed out in the sketch of his life in Chapter Two, Smith was raised in a Scottish Presbyterian home, his father being remembered as having been a zealous churchman and his mother being known as a "deeply religious" person who lived almost as long as her son and between whom there was a "particularly close and tender tie".[8]

His favorite teacher in college, Francis Hutcheson, was a Christian who, in addition to his regular lectures in Moral Philosophy, conducted a Sunday class on "Christian evidences". Smith signed the Westminster Confession before the Presbytery of Glasgow, lectured among other things on natural theology, and recommended a divinity student as his successor in the Chair of Moral Philosophy at the University of Glasgow; and his academic colleagues were professing Christians who thought so much of him that they eventually elected him Rector of the University.[9]

2. In Thought

That Smith was a theist there can be no reasonable doubt. We have not only specific assertions to this effect by his principal biographer[10] but also many evidences in his writing. However, it is a theism with a strong deistic flavor — that is, a theism in whose concept of God the characteristic of transcendence is especially emphasized. The most typical names used to refer to the Deity (which word appears frequently itself, as does "God") are "Author of Nature", "Director of Nature", "Creator", "Conductor of the Universe", "great Physician of Nature", and Nature's "all-wise

Architect".[11] Thus the Divine's chief concern is thought of as the administration of the "great system" of the universe which has been created and sustained by Him from the beginning — a fact often forgotten by man who is inclined to attribute to "the wisdom of man" what is in reality due to "the wisdom of God". He is also the "Judge of the world" and the "Judge of hearts" before whose "unerring tribunal" men's motives as well as their actions will ultimately be tested. Fortunately for man, both benevolence and wisdom are His chief characteristics. Doubt of His existence brings the bleakest misery even to the most benevolent men, Smith writes, whereas confidence of it creates the highest joy:

> "This universal benevolence (of the most virtuous men), how noble and generous soever, can be the source of no solid happiness to any man who is not thoroughly convinced that all the inhabitants of the universe, the meanest as well as the greatest, are under the immediate care and protection of that great, benevolent, and all-wise Being, who directs all the movements of nature, and who is determined, by his own unalterable perfections, to maintain in it at all times the greatest possible quantity of happiness. To this universal benevolence, on the contrary, the very suspicion of a fatherless world must be the most melancholy of all reflections; from the thought that all the unknown regions of infinite and incomprehensible space may be filled with nothing but endless misery and wretchedness. All the splendour of the highest prosperity can never enlighten the gloom with which so dreadful an idea

must necessarily overshadow the imagination; nor, in a wise and virtuous man, can all the sorrow of the most afflicting adversity ever dry up the joy which necessarily springs from the habitual and thorough conviction of the truth of the contrary system."[12]

As for man's response, Smith speaks with approval of "that pure and rational religion, free from every mixture of absurdity, imposture, or fanaticism, such as wise men have in all ages wished to see established"; and he disliked all "enthusiasm and superstition", which he regarded as "poison".[13]

He refers specifically to Christianity only occasionally in his writings, but he does refer to Christ as "our Saviour" and the earlier editions of the "Theory" included a passage on the atonement, included as Appendix #2.[14] Whether fuller treatment was given in the first part of his lecture series, in which, as we recall, he dealt with "the proofs of the being and attributes of God, and those principles of the human mind upon which religion is founded",[15] is an interesting subject for speculation.

His close friendship with Hume and great admiration for Voltaire doubtless strengthened his free-thinking tendencies; and certainly he did not "go along with" (to use a phrase which appears repeatedly in his earlier work) much that was associated with the established Church of England of the time nor with the Church of Rome.[16] In general, he opposed establishment *per se,* as he did a permanent monopoly in any field, believing that a rivalry between various small sects was good both for society and for religion itself.[17] However, he maintained his membership in

the Scottish Presbyterian Church, which, though established, seemed to him to have prospered spiritually
through maintaining a clergy who were not seekers of
wealth or position and who were on the whole a
"learned, decent, independent and respectable set of
men".[18]

Emphasizing the ethical aspect of religion, he regarded it as an insult to God to consider as of prime
importance in men's activities and attitudes toward
Him what can best be compared to "the attendance
and adulation" offered earthly rulers by assiduous
courtiers.[19] Consequently, he opposed "the futile mor-
tifications of the monastery" and he regarded as of
only minor importance "the duties of devotions, the
public and private worship of the Deity".[20]   Rather,
with ideas and phrases which call to mind similar ones
from the teachings of the Prophets and of Christ, he
writes:

> "Wherever the natural principles of religion are
> not corrupted by the factious and party zeal of
> some worthless cabal" the first duty it requires is
> "to fulfill all the obligations of morality . . . men
> are not taught to regard frivolous observances as
> more immediate duties of religion than acts of
> justice and beneficence, and to imagine that by
> sacrifices and ceremonies and vain supplications
> they can bargain with the Deity for fraud, and
> perfidy, and violence."[21]

"To obey the will of the Deity is the first rule of
duty"; but this is not easy, and the virtuous man as he
tries to imitate the work of the "divine artist" will
inevitably feel "the imperfect success of his best endeavours" and see "with grief and affliction in how

many different features the mortal copy falls short of the immortal original". And Smith continues:

> "He (the virtuous man) remembers, with concern and humiliation, how often, from want of attention, from want of judgment, from want of temper, he has, both in words and actions, both in conduct and conversation, violated the exact rules of perfect propriety, and has so far departed from that model, according to which he wished to fashion his own character and conduct."[22]

However, like a good soldier he should submit himself and his best to the will of the great Commander — leaving the ultimate outcome to Him and accepting not only willingly but with joy whatever sacrifice is asked for the sake of the good of the whole — ideas which appear clearly in this characteristic passage:

> "The wise and virtuous man is at all times willing that his own private interest should be sacrificed to the public interest of his own particular order of society. He is at all times willing, too, that the interest of this order of society should be sacrificed to the greater interest of the state or sovereignty of which it is only a subordinate part: he should, therefore, be equally willing that all those inferior interests should be sacrificed to the greater interest of the universe, to the interest of that great society of all sensible and intelligent beings, of which God Himself is the immediate administrator and director . . .
>
> "Nor does this magnanimous resignation to the will of the great Director of the universe seem in any respect beyond the reach of human nature. Good soldiers, who both love and trust their gen-

eral, frequently march with more gaiety and alacrity to the forlorn station, from which they never expect to return, than they would to one where there was neither difficulty nor danger. In marching to the latter they could feel no other sentiment than that of the dullness of ordinary duty — in marching to the former, they feel that they are making the noblest exertion which it is possible for man to make. They know that their general would not have ordered them upon this station had it not been necessary for the safety of the army, for the success of the war; they cheerfully sacrifice their own little systems to the prosperity of a greater system; they take an affectionate leave of their comrades, to whom they wish all happiness and success, and march out, not only with submissive obedience, but often with shouts of the most joyful exultation, to that fatal but splendid and honourable station to which they are appointed.

"No conductor of an army can deserve more unlimited trust, more ardent and zealous affection, than the great Conductor of the universe."[23]

Religion, thus, for Smith, would seem, in an explicit sense, to be primarily a matter of intellect and of will. The former leads him to a general theistic interpretation of the world and the latter to a high sense of duty toward the "great Director of the universe" and towards other men. Emotion and "enthusiasm" in religion are highly distrusted — except, as indicated in the above quotation, in the performance of duty. And ecclesiasticism is for him at best a deplorable necessity.[24]

C. Smith's Relationship to Christianity — Implicitly

Our concern in this section is to examine certain presuppositions which would seem to underly Smith's thought — assumptions which are not always specifically connected with Christianity in particular, or even with religion in general, but which nevertheless seem to stem from a Christian approach to life. This, at any rate, is the judgment of the writer, and the reader is invited to regard it as a hypothesis to be considered, recalling the first section of this chapter with reference to the meaning of the terms "religion" and "Christianity" as here understood.

1. The Concept of Order and Structure in the Universe

That the universe in which we find ourselves is a cosmos — an ordered system, not a chaos — is a basic assumption for Smith that is not only implied in many of his ideas but explicitly expressed again and again in his writings. This is especially evident in the "Theory" but it is likewise the case with respect to the "Inquiry".

a. The "Invisible Hand"

One of the evidences most frequently referred to is his reference to the guiding and beneficent "invisible hand", which, when not interfered with, tends to fit the activities of individual men into a pattern favorable to the welfare of society as a whole. Both his principal writings have passages mentioning this ordering force, the more familiar being that of the "Inquiry":

"As every individual, therefore, endeavours as much as he can both to employ his capital in the support of domestic industry, and so to direct that industry that its produce may be of the greatest value; every individual necessarily labours to render the annual revenue of the society as great as he can. He generally, indeed, neither intends to promote the public interest, nor knows how much he is promoting it. By preferring the support of domestic to that of foreign industry, he intends only his own security; and by directing that industry in such a manner as its produce may be of the greatest value, he intends only his own gain, and he is in this, as in many other cases, led by an invisible hand to promote an end which was no part of his intention."[25]

b. Nature

Another closely related evidence (at times, seemingly, almost synonymous with "the invisible hand") is the idea of Nature as an ordering, guiding influence. At times the concept seems rather impersonal in Smith's thought, as when he speaks of "natural" rates of wages and "natural" prices, the "powers of nature in agricultural production", or of the real value of corn's being stamped upon it by "the nature of things".[26]

More often, however, especially in the "Theory", Nature seems to be regarded as a personal — or perhaps better, personified — force which makes use of impersonal mechanism and laws; and in these cases the word is often capitalized. For example, he speaks of "the mechanism by which nature produces" a certain effect, or again, of "the reward which Nature bestows on good behaviour under misfortune" as being "exactly proportioned to the degree of that good behaviour", saying of one in such a situation:

"When he follows that view which honour and dignity point out to him, Nature does not, indeed, leave him without a recompense. He enjoys his own complete self-approbation, and the applause of every candid and impartial spectator. By her unalterable laws, however, he still suffers; and the recompense which she bestows, though very considerably, is not sufficient completely to compensate the sufferings which those laws inflict. Neither is it fit that it should. If it did completely compensate them, he could, from self-interest, have no motive for avoiding an accident which must necessarily diminish his utility both to himself and to society; and Nature, from her parental care of both, meant that he should anxiously avoid all such accidents."[27]

Elsewhere Nature appears as seeking to produce concord through the teaching of sympathy — an important concept in Smith's system of thought, as we have seen:

"In order to produce this concord, as Nature teaches the spectators to assume the circumstances of the person principally concerned, so she teaches this last in some measure to assume those of the spectators. As they are continually placing themselves in his situation, and then conceiving emotions similar to what he feels; so he is constantly placing himself in theirs, and thence conceiving some degree of that coolness about his own fortune, with which he is sensible that they will view it. As they are constantly considering what they themselves would feel, if they were actually the sufferers, so he is constantly led to imagine in what manner he would be affected if he was only one of the spectators of his own situation. As their sympathy makes them look at it in some measure with his eyes, so his sympathy makes him look at it, in some measure, with theirs, especially when in their presence, and acting under their observation; and, as the reflected passion which he thus conceives is much weaker than the original one, it necessarily abates the violence of what he felt before he came into their presence, before he began to recollect in what manner they would be affected by it, and to view his situation in this candid and impartial light."[28]

c. Evil and the Result of Virtue

Smith's confidence in the orderliness of the universe is so great that he argues at times that evil is only a part — viewed from an inadequate perspective — of a more ultimate good, which, if fully known, would be the desire of every good man.[29]

He argues, too, that in this great order virtue ultimately receives its proper reward, usually in this life:

"What reward is most proper for promoting the practice of truth, justice, and humanity? — The confidence, the esteem, and love of those we live with. It is not in being rich that truth and justice would rejoice, but in being trusted and believed, recompenses which those virtues must always acquire."[30]

So, "kindness is the parent of kindness", for "Nature, which formed men for that mutual kindness so necessary for their happiness, renders every man the pecul-

iar object of kindness to the persons to whom he himself has been kind . . .

> "No benevolent man ever lost altogether the
> fruits of his benevolence. If he does not always
> gather them from the persons from whom he
> ought to have gathered them, he seldom fails to
> gather them, and with tenfold increase, from other
> people."[31]

Evil-doing, Smith maintains, is also properly rewarded
ultimately, for "as every man doeth, so it shall be done
to him",[32] the total process thus serving the virtue of
justice.

Smith was one of those who took great pleasure in
the perfection of beautiful and grand systems and in
the "beauty of order" wherever he found it; and he regarded the idea of God as the source of the orderly
universe as "of all objects of human contemplation by
far the most sublime", every other thought appearing
"mean in comparison".[33] It was because of his belief in
this universal order that he could and did speak con-
fidently of such things as right and truth and reality.[34]

2. *The Value of Men and Society*

Both explicitly and implicitly Smith tells his readers
of his conviction of the importance of individuals and
of society. It is this fundamental concern which supplies the basic motivation behind much of his work —
his effort to understand and explain the process of
sympathy, for example, and his challenging of the
dominant financial and commercial interests of his day
in the cause of popular welfare and justice, to which
"the most sacred regard is due".[35] His biographer Rae
speaks of the "deep love of justice and humanity which

animated Smith beyond his fellows and ran as warmly
through his conversation in private life as we see it run
through his published writings", and he continues:

"Smith was always vigorous and weighty in his
denunciation of wrong, and so impatient of anything in the nature of indifference or palliation towards it, that he could scarcely feel at ease in the
presence of the palliator. 'We can breathe more
freely now,' he once said when a person of that
sort had just left the company; 'that man has no
indignation in him.' "[36]

a. On Injustice

His choice of words to describe injustice is an evidence of his own capacity for moral indignation; and
it is in the treatise on what is so often regarded as the
cold and impersonal subject of economics that this
quality is most often manifested. He characterizes as
"vile" the selfish maxim of "all for ourselves and nothing for other people" which seems to have been followed by "the masters of mankind" in every age;[37] and
later on we read of the "savage injustice of the treatment by Europeans of the American natives", and
again, of the "impertinent jealousy" and "mean rapacity" of monopolistic merchants and manufacturers,
and of the "ancient evil" of the "the violence and injustice of the rulers of mankind".[38] He is also indignant
at any "grievous tax on the poor people" and regards
monopolistic imperialism as "invidious and malignant";
and, as already noted, he condemns some laws for
which monopolies are responsible as so cruel that they
may be said to have been "written in blood".[39]

b. The Worth of Humanity

Smith speaks, positively, of "the most sacred rights of mankind" and maintains that the sovereign (or state) owes "justice and equality of treatment . . . to all the different orders of subjects"; and he opposed the entailing of estates as being "founded upon the most absurd of all suppositions, the supposition that every successive generation of men have not an equal right to the earth and what it possesses".[40]

"Humanity", he defines as "the exquisite fellow-feeling which the spectator entertains with the sentiments of the person principally concerned, so as to grieve for their sufferings, to resent their injuries, and to rejoice at their good fortune", and as such it receives high praise.[41] That he himself practiced this virtue is evidenced by the discovery after his death that though his income was large and his scale of living moderate he left a very small estate, due to his having given away "large sums in secret charity".[42]

Man as man, then, is of great worth for Smith — the ultimate ground for his value being the fact that the "all-wise Author of Nature" has made man "after his own image" and "appointed him his vice-regent upon earth".[43] He is related to the Divine, too, by the presence within his breast of the *impartial spectator* — "reason, principle, conscience" — the "demigod" who guides him away from the wrong and toward the right:

> "It is he who, whenever we are about to act so as to affect the happiness of others, calls to us, with a voice capable of astonishing the most presumptuous of our passions, that we are but one of the multitude, in no respect better than any other

in it; and that when we prefer ourselves so shamefully and so blindly to others, we become the proper objects of resentment, abhorrence, and execration. It is from him only that we learn the real littleness of ourselves, and of whatever relates to ourselves, and the natural misrepresentations of self-love can be corrected only by the eye of this impartial spectator. It is he who shows us the propriety of generosity and deformity of injustice; the propriety of resigning the greatest interests of our own for the yet greater interests of others; and the deformity of doing the smallest injury to another in order to obtain the greatest benefit to ourselves."[44]

As this quotation makes clear, it is not just one individual or a few lofty ones that are of value, but all men. "By the wisdom of Nature," he says, "the happiness of every innocent man is . . . rendered holy, consecrated, and hedged around against the approach of every other man; not to be wantonly trod upon, not even to be, in any respect, ignorantly and involuntarily violated, without requiring some expiation, some atonement in proportion to the greatness of such undesigned violation."[45]

All men are held, then, to be of worth as individuals and also in their togetherness as society. Smith puts great emphasis on the social character of man, as being fitted by Nature for society, as we have seen; for "how selfish soever man may be supposed, there are evidently some principles in his nature which interest him in the fortunes of others, and render their happiness necessary for him".[46]

"Nature, when she formed man for society, endowed him with an original desire to please, and
an original aversion to offend his brethren. She
taught him to feel pleasure in their favourable,
and pain in their unfavourable regard. She rendered their approbation most flattering and most
agreeable to him for its own sake; and their disap-
probation most mortifying and most offensive."
Moreover, and yet more important, "Nature . . .
has endowed him, not only with a desire of being
approved of, but with a desire of being what ought
to be approved of; or of being what he himself approves of in other men."[47]

To raise and support the "immense fabric of human
society" seems to him to be "the peculiar and darling
care of nature"; and it is for this reason that justice,
"the main pillar that upholds the whole edifice" is so
important. For man, despite his relation to the Divine,
is made "of coarse clay" and is full of "insolence" and
pride, both individual and social; and people are so
much of the time so concerned with their own interests
and "feel so little for another, with whom they have
no particular connection, in comparison with what they
feel for themselves", and "the misery of one, who is
merely their fellow creature, is of so little importance
to them in comparison even of a small conveniency of
their own", that "if this principle (justice) did not
stand up within them in his defence, and overawe
them into a respect for his innocence . . . a man would
enter an assembly of men as he enters a den of lions".[48]
However, man has such a "natural love for society" and
"the orderly and flourishing state of society is so agreeable to him" that the principle of justice does "stand

up within him"; and he is so opposed to the disorder and confusion which result from injustice — so harmful to the real interests of all, including his own — that he is willing to resort to the most rigorous means to prevent it.

> "If he cannot restrain it by gentle and fair means, he must bear it down by force and violence, at any rate must put a stop to its further progress."[49]

Moreover, injustice is such an offense against the values incarnated in men and society that "nature teaches us to hope, and religion, we suppose, authorizes us to expect, that it will be punished in a life to come".[50]

c. Persons Before System

Despite Smith's love of system and orderliness, the value of persons comes first for him, and he inveighs against the type of reformer who lets his love of system lead him to treat people like chessmen. Such a one, he says, is apt to be "very wise in his own conceit" and "so enamoured with the supposed beauty of his own ideal plan of government, that he cannot suffer the smallest deviation from it", forgetting that in "the great chess-board of human society every single piece has a principle of motion of its own". Continuing, he gives this counsel of moderation to reformers and statesmen:

> "Some general, and even systematical, idea of the perfection of policy and law may no doubt be necessary for directing the views of the statesman. But to insist upon establishing all at once, and in spite of all opposition, everything which that idea

may seem to require, must often be the highest degree of arrogance. It is to erect his own judgment into the supreme standard of right and wrong. It is to fancy himself the only wise and worthy man in the commonwealth, and that his fellow-citizens should accomodate themselves to him, and not he to them. It is upon this account that of all political speculators, sovereign princes are by far the most dangerous."[51]

Man is no angel in Smith's view, as his emphasis on the fact of injustice, and the need for punishing it, makes clear. Nevertheless, the being, just rights, and happiness of our fellows are worthy of a "sacred and religious regard" on our part if our aim is to be "innocent and just".[52] And coupled with this just and benevolent attitude should go the right amount of self-esteem and the highest personal virtue if we are to be worthy of being treated with respect by others.[53]

3. The Ideas of Purpose and Progress in the Universe

The ideas of purpose and progress quite naturally belong together in that progress is really one of the possible ways by which purpose may be realized, and purpose is implicit in the concept of progress, whether or not clearly expressed. Both are assumptions, whether as open or covert beliefs. They certainly cannot be proved true or false in any empirical sense, any more than can the basic order and intelligibility of the universe or the real value of man and society, though reasons can, of course, be given for all of them. Belief in progress is, in the words of J. B. Bury, "an act of faith";[54] and this would also seem true of belief in purpose at work in the world (in addition to that of human beings).

a. Toward General Happiness and Perfection

Smith's goals, already noted, of general happiness and perfection he conceives of as part of the basic scheme of things as supported by Nature and the Divine. We read, for example, of the "plan of providence . . . the scheme which the Author of Nature has established for the happiness and perfection of the world".[55] This idea is quite different from that of purely individual happiness as the central aim in a philosophy of life; he speaks, for example, of Epicurus's philosophy as being for this reason "altogether inconsistent" with his own,[56] with the latter's emphasis on the seeking of three-fold virtue, of which prudence, with its individual-centeredness, is but a part, and the lowest part.

b. Beyond This Life

Our concern, Smith holds, is not only with this life but also with that to come, where our progress here will be measured and where "exact justice will be done to every man" before the tribunal of that "all-seeing Judge of the word whose eye can never be deceived, and whose judgments can never be perverted".

> "A firm confidence in the unerring rectitude of this great tribunal, before which his (the wrongly punished innocent man's) innocence is in due time to be declared, and his virtue to be finally rewarded, can alone support him under the weakness and despondency of his own mind, under the perturbation and astonishment of the man within the breast, whom nature has set up as, in this life, the great guardian, not only of his innocence but of his tranquillity.

"Our happiness in this life is thus, upon many occasions, dependent upon the humble hope and expectation of a life to come; a hope and expectation deeply rooted in human nature, which can alone illumine the dreary prospect of its continually approaching mortality, and maintain its cheerfulness under all the heaviest calamities to which, from the disorders of this life, it may sometimes be exposed."[57]

So it is our hope that "the great Author of our nature will himself execute hereafter, what all the principles which he has given us for the direction of our conduct prompt us to attempt even here; that he will complete the plan which he himself has thus taught us to begin; and will, in a life to come, render to everyone according to the works which he has performed in this world".[58] Thus the idea of "another and better world" — "a world of more candour, humanity, and justice, than the present" — reinforces the belief of purpose in this life.[59]

c. Nature as Ally

Smith sees progress towards the realizing of the purposes of life as a real possibility, with Nature as a potent aid. "In every part of the universe," he writes, "we observe means adjusted with the nicest artifice to the ends which they are intended to produce."[60]

"Mankind are endowed with a desire of those ends, and an aversion to the contrary . . . Hunger, thirst, the passion which unites the two sexes, the love of pleasure, and the dread of pain, prompt us to apply those means for their own sakes, and without any consideration of their tendency to those beneficent ends which the great Director of Nature intended to produce by them."[61]

And so, too, we find Nature undergirding in like fashion the higher levels of virtue — justice and benevolence, as well as prudence — primarily through the spirit of fair play and the love of both approval and of being worthy of approval.

". . . Every part of Nature, when attentively surveyed, equally demonstrates the providential care of its Author; and we may admire the wisdom and goodness of God even in the weakness and folly of men."[62]

In Brief Summary

Smith's life and thought indicate, therefore, what may be spoken of as a "steeping" in Christianity — thought of here, as noted, as the total Judeo-Hellenic-Christian heritage — especially the ethical aspects. This, together with the influence of 18th century "enlightenment" emphases plus his own thinking and experience, resulted in an approach which might well be described as a deistically flavored, ethical theism of Christian orientation.

REFERENCES

[1] Becker, (op. cit.), p. 14, quoting Bertrand Russell.
[2] Isaiah 6:1-9.
[3] See italicized definition.
[4] Genesis, Chapter 1, expresses this idea seven times in a kind of refrain — Verses 4, 10, 12, 18, 21, 25 and 31.
[5] This is, of course, "Logos" in the original Greek of the New Testament, a term of real importance in Greek philosophy as well.
[6] John 14:17, 15:26 and 16:13.

[7] Mannheim, Karl, "Ideology and Utopia", New York, Harcourt, Brace and Company, 1936, p. 80.

[8] Rae, (op. cit.), p. 1; also Scott, "Adam Smith as Student and Professor", (op. cit.), pp. 20 and 64; also Hirst, (op. cit.), p. 8.

[9] Rae, (op. cit.), pp. 9 and 60; Scott, (op. cit.), pp. 138-9; and Rae, (op. cit.), pp. 169 and 410. Smith discontinued the Sunday class when he assumed the Moral Philosophy chair.

[10] Rae, (op. cit.), pp. 129 and 313.

[11] "Theory", (op. cit.), pp., in order, 232, 235, 109, 110, 241, 347 and 422.

[12] Ibid., pp., in order, 348, 127, 176, 153 and 345-6.

[13] "Inquiry" (op. cit.), pp. 745 and 748.

[14] "Theory" (op. cit.), pp. 27 and 253 and Appendix #2.

[15] Rae, (op. cit.), pp. 54-5.

[16] "Inquiry" (op. cit.), pp. 745 and 754 and 759-60; also 528 and 541.

[17] Ibid., p. 744. In this connection Smith expresses approval of the situation in Pennsylvania under the leadership of the Quakers, where, with the law favoring no sect more than another, there appears to be "philosophical good temper and moderation". Ibid., p. 745.

[18] Ibid., pp. 761-2.

[19] "Theory" (op. cit.), pp. 188-90.

[20] Ibid., pp. 189 and 188.

[21] Ibid., p. 242. One is vividly reminded by this passage of such ideas from the Old Testament Prophets and from Jesus as are expressed in the following — with which Smith was doubtless familiar:

— Amos 5:21-24: "I hate, I despise your feasts, and I take no delight in your solemn assemblies (says the Lord). Even though you offer me your burnt offerings and cereal offerings, I will not accept them, and the peace offerings of your fatted beasts I will not look upon. Take away from me the noise of your songs; to the melody of your harps I will not listen. But let justice roll down like waters, and righteousness like an everflowing stream."

— Hosea 6:6: "For I desire steadfast love and not sacrifice, the knowledge of God, rather than burnt offerings."

— Isaiah 1:11, 16-17: "What to me is the multitude of your sacrifices? says the Lord . . . Wash yourselves; make yourselves clean; remove the evil of your doings from before my eyes; cease to do evil, learn to do good; seek justice, correct oppression; defend the fatherless, plead for the widow."

— Micah 6:6-8: "With what shall I come before the Lord, and bow myself before God on high? Shall I come before him with burnt offerings, with calves a year old? Will the Lord be pleased with thousands of rams, with ten thousands of rivers of oil? Shall I give my first-born for my transgression, the fruit of my body for the sin of my soul? He has showed you, O man, what is good; and what does the Lord require of you but to do justice, and to love kindness, and to walk humbly with your God?"

— Jeremiah 7:9-11: "Will you steal, murder, commit adultery, swear falsely, burn incense to Baal, and go after other gods that you have not known, and then come and stand in this house, which is called by my name, and say, 'We are delivered!' — only to go on doing all these abominations? Has this house, which is called by my name, become a den of robbers in your eyes?"

— Matthew 23:23-7: "Woe to you, scribes and Pharisees, hypocrites! for you tithe mint and dill and cummin, and have neglected the weightier matters of the law, justice and mercy and faith; these you ought to have done, without neglecting the others. You blind guides, straining out a gnat and swallowing a camel! Woe to you scribes and Pharisees, hypocrites! for you cleanse the outside of the cup and of the plate, but inside they are full of extortion and rapacity. You blind Pharisee! first cleanse the inside of the cup and of the plate, that the outside also may be clean. Woe to you, scribes and Pharisees, hypocrites! for you are like whitewashed tombs, which outwardly appear beautiful, but within they are full of dead men's bones and all uncleanness. So you also outwardly appear righteous to men, but within you are full of hypocrisy and iniquity."

[22] Ibid., pp. 251 and 364.

[23] Ibid., pp. 346-7.

[24] Were this all that could be said, this book would not have been written; what follows is clearly needed to give life and vitality to the picture.

[25] "Inquiry", p. 423. Recall Chapter Three, Section 2. i.

[26] Ibid., pp., in order, 55, 344, and 482.

[27] "Theory", pp. 135 and 207-8.

[28] Ibid., pp. 23-4. Recall in this connection Chapter Three, Section 2. b., on sympathy and also the material on benevolence in the following section, especially the quotation with footnote reference #43.

[29] This statement needs to be considered in relationship to what follows, especially his condemnation of injustice in all its forms; for Smith can certainly not be accused of indifference to anti-social conduct! But see "Theory", p. 346, for this line of thought when Smith is dealing with the concept of universal "system". There is, in fact, an inadequately faced tension between his metaphysics and his ethics in this regard.

[30] Ibid., p. 236.

[31] Ibid., p. 331.

[32] Ibid., p. 117.   See also footnote #50 below and what it refers to.

[33] Ibid., pp. 265-6 and 347.   Recall earlier reference in Chapter Three, Section 2. c., footnoted quotation #49.

[34] Ibid., p. 21.

[35] Ibid., p. 249.

[36] Rae, (op. cit.), p. 245.

[37] "Inquiry", pp. 388-9.

[38] Ibid., pp. 416 and 460.

[39] Ibid., pp. 541, 561 and 612.   Recall fuller quotation, with footnote reference #82 in Chapter Three.

[40] Ibid., pp., in order, 549, 618 and 363.

[41] "Theory" (op. cit.), p. 274.

[42] Rae, (op. cit.), p. 437.

[43] "Theory" (op. cit.), p. 185.

[44] Ibid., pp., in order, 185, 194, 187, and 194.   Recall earlier reference in Chapter Three in material with footnotes #32-3.

[45] Ibid., p. 155.

[46] Ibid., p. 3.   (These are the opening words of the book.)

[47] Ibid., p. 170.

[48] Ibid., pp.   125 and 230; and "Inquiry" (op. cit.), pp., in order, 751, 365 and 582; and (longer quotation) "Theory", pp. 125-6.

[49] Ibid., ("Theory"), p. 127.

[50] Ibid., p. 132.   Recall earlier passages dealing with justice and injustice in Chapter Three, Section 2. c. and in this chapter, Section 2. a. and 3. b.

[51] Ibid., pp. 342-3.

[52] Ibid., pp. 319-20.

[53] Ibid., pp. 382-3 and 436-7.

[54] Bury, J. B., "The Idea of Progress", New York, The Macmillan Co., 1932, p. 4.

[55] "Theory" (op. cit.), p. 235.

[56] Ibid., pp. 431-6.

[57] Ibid., p. 187.

[58] Ibid., p. 240.

[59] "Inquiry" (op. cit.), p. 740 and "Theory" (op. cit.), p. 176.

[60] Ibid., ("Theory"), p. 126.

[61] Ibid., pp. 109-10.

[62] Ibid., p. 153.

CHAPTER FIVE

SMITH AND TODAY'S ETHICAL PROBLEMS

Smith has been, as it were, "historified" by most and is referred to nearly always exclusively for certain ideas set forth in his "Wealth of Nations". As a moral philosopher he has been virtually forgotten. His "Theory of the Moral Sentiments" is obtainable only with luck through second-hand bookstores when old libraries are sold; yet it was to the revision of this work that he gave his last years and it is in the realm of ethics that his ideas would seem to have the greatest continuing relevance. Perhaps this has already become clear to one who has read this far; but express dealing with the question of just what he has to say to our time would appear to be worth explicit treatment. This was promised in Chapter One and his ideas will be considered in this chapter in relation to the problems enumerated there, though with a slight variation in order.

Thoughtful churchmen may well find such a process of special significance, for, as we have seen, much of Smith's inspiration comes from Christianity, both with respect to his explicit teaching and to his implicit presuppositions of the order and structure to be found in the universe, the value of men and of society, and the reality of purpose and progress in life.[1] The fact that these ideas are expressed chiefly in non-ecclesiastical terms is a major asset, as it requires fresh thinking and also because it opens up new possibilities of communication with non-churchmen, with the values of a fuller flow of ideas in both directions.

A. *The Individual and Society*

Living in a period which is widely considered as the century of individualism throughout Europe, Smith, while thoroughly aware of the importance of the individual, nevertheless maintained, as we have seen, that human beings are inextricably interdependent, that man needs society for his full development, serving as it does as a kind of mirror in which he may view his strengths and weaknesses of character.[2]

This interdependence works most effectively, of course, when as in a healthy, happy family mutual assistance is based on love and gratitude and friendship and esteem[3] — hence the first-rate ethical importance of maximizing these qualities in our day as well as his; but it can also function, at a lower level, on the foundation of the concept of utility supported by a systematized exchange of functions and goods.[4] Here, too, we see the ethical importance of developing and maintaining the fullest opportunity for such exchange.

However, the *indispensable* ingredient is justice, in its simplest form the prevention of mutual injury. Injustice, so conceived, would before long bring society down in collapse like a house whose main support is removed. One can conceive of a social order without beneficence but not without justice.[5] Here, clearly, is an ethical base for an unflagging zeal to support the most vital system of laws, police and courts, dedicated to the protection of the rights of every individual.

Going back, then, to our first question in Chapter One, "Is there an irreconcilable conflict between them (the individual and society) requiring an ultimate choice between more or less rugged individualism and collectivism?" No, says Smith, they are, when properly analyzed, mutually sustaining — when based on justice. But is this not utopian? It is obvious to any student of society, whether in the 20th or the 18th century, that we have anything but full justice — a glance at any day's newspaper making this painfully clear. However, Smith was no perfectionist. He was rather, as it were, an acute societal physician, vividly aware of the fact, and broad-scale incidence, of disease; but he was able to operate and prescribe because of his awareness of an underlying principle of health provided by Nature to overcome the harm caused by much of man's foolishness and bad conduct.[6] This principle is *sympathy*, through which we are able, to a significant extent at least, to place ourselves, with the aid of the imagination, in the situation of others and then, with the aid of conscience, act accordingly.

We may or may not go along all the way with Smith's concept of "the impartial spectator" as virtually a "demigod" within the breast; but who would deny that there is that within each of us that enables us to see, to an appreciable extent at any rate, that the interests of others as well as his own are important? As Smith makes so vividly clear it would be a human freak who could face mankind and openly maintain the primacy of his own interests over all others; and it is fortunately rare also to find one who is not incensed by the violation of "fair play".[7] Hence our support of policemen and courts, even if we ourselves are brought to trial, and our readiness to serve as jurymen or in other activities which undergird the judicial process.

Perhaps Smith's view as here understood might be diagramed as follows with the individual and the community, or society, as the two poles of an axis,

with vital influence flowing from each to the other and
with the welfare of each being indispensable to the
full development of the other.

Individual o——«————»——o Society

B. Justice and Love

Probably no question has received more searching
attention by ethicists in our day. Both individuals
and conferences have given it their attention with
reference to every area of human relations. There
have been those who stress the primacy of "justice" —
variously defined — with love as a nice but not too
important additional factor. Others have made "love"
— also variously defined — the very heart of the matter,
with justice regarded as either of secondary importance, or, in some cases, as virtually an alternative.
However, the "main line" has involved the effort to
relate the two creatively, as can be seen in the re-
spected Oxford Conference Report on the Church and
the Economic Order.[8]

It is at this point, in the effort to relate the two
concept-practices effectively, that Smith has one of his
most vital contributions to make, as significant in our
day as in his own. He does so by bringing in a third
factor and relating all three in his concept of the good
life or "virtue". We have already examined this three-
fold concept,[9] but its implications merit further attention. The basis, we recall, is *"prudence"* — the care of
the health, fortune, rank and reputation of the individual himself and, by extension, that of the individual's
family. His contribution here is not so much the recognition of this force as an actual factor in the human

situation but in the treatment of it as positively good
rather than as something to be, in effect, apologized
for. To be sure, it is regarded as an aspect of the
good life which can command only "cold esteem"
rather than warm admiration; but still it is, Smith
maintains, a genuine part of virtue. We may well contrast with this view the myriads of sermons preached
and essays written on "selflessness" which seemingly
overlook the Old Testament and New Testament teachings to love one's neighbor *as oneself*[10] and Paul's
castigation of those who don't look after those of their
own household:

> "If any one does not provide for his relatives,
> and especially for his own family, he has disowned
> the faith and is worse than an unbeliever."[11]

It would seem that if not only the inevitability but the
value of responsible concern for self and family could
be clearly recognized, a good deal of the unreality of
much moralizing and the hypocrisy of much action
could be avoided.

However this, we also recall, is only the beginning
— the lowest rung of the ladder. The activities origi-
nating in prudence must be kept within the bonds set
by "*justice*". We have noted how centrally important
this is in Smith's thought, being for him the basis of
civil government and, indeed, the chief support of the
whole structure of society.[12] We have noted, too,
that it has in its most rudimentary sense what may be
spoken of as a negative aspect — the abstention from,
prevention of, and, where needed, punishment for injury to others. Each is not only free but encouraged
to run as hard as he can in the race for wealth and
other advantages so long as he does not interfere with

the like freedom of others, for this is a "violation of fair play" which cannot be allowed.[13] This brings us to the other side of the coin (of justice) — the positive aspect of "fair play", whose rules Smith compares to the rules of grammar in relationship to good composition; and it was to their exposition that he devoted the third division of his lectures, with the unfulfilled intention of writing a major treatise on the subject.[14]

A strikingly similar treatment of justice as a two-aspect virtue is found in the Oxford Conference report already referred to — a basic document for all later Ecumenical Movement thinking in this area:

"The principle of justice has both a positive and negative significance.

"Negatively, principles of justice restrain evil and the evil-doer. They must therefore become embodied in a system of coercion which prevent men from doing what sinful ambition, pride, lust, and greed might prompt them to do . . . It cannot be assumed that the practice of Christian love will ever obviate the necessity for coercive political and economic arrangements.

"The laws of justice are not purely negative (however). They are not merely 'dykes against sin'. The political and economic structure of society is also the mechanical skeleton which carries the organic element in society. Forms of production and methods of cooperation may serve the cause of human brotherhood by serving and extending the principle of love beyond the sphere of purely personal relations.

"The commandment of love therefore always presents possibilities for individuals beyond the

requirements of economic and social institutions
. . . The man who is in Christ knows a higher
obligation, which transcends the requirements of
justice — the obligation of a love which is the
fulfillment of the law.

"The love which is the fulfillment of the law is,
however, no substitute for law, for institutions, or
for systems . . . Undue emphasis upon the higher
possibilities of love in personal relations, within
the limits of a given system of justice or an established social structure, may tempt Christians to
allow individual acts of charity to become a screen
for injustice and a substitute for justice. Christianity becomes socially futile if it does not rec-
ognize that love must will justice and that the
Christian is under an obligation to secure the
best possible social and economic structure, in so
far as such structure is determined by human
decision."[15]

Smithian ethics undergirds such an analysis in an
effective manner, not only with respect to the two
aspects of justice but also in the treatment of justice
and love as the following considerations indicate.

Centrally important as justice is in Smith's thought
it does not bring us to the heights of full virtue; but
with prudence, properly limited, it forms the essential
foundation on which the peaks rest and from which
they soar. The peak-area — or the highest rung of the
ladder — is what Smith terms, interchangeably, "*benevolence*" or "*beneficence*", comprising the qualities of
humanity, sensibility, magnanimity, generosity, charity,
and kindness; he also includes in this list what really
summarizes the group of characteristics — "love for

others".[16] "Good will" and "good action" (the literal
meanings, of course, of "benevolence" and "beneficence") combined are thus conceived as expressing
themselves in such attitudes and actions as listed
above. In considering them one is almost inevitably
reminded of some of St. Paul's phrases in the 13th
chapter of 1st Corinthians as he seeks to express the
outworking of the core Biblical ethical principle — that
of "love" ("agape" in Greek):

St. Paul	Smith
"Love" — "is patient and kind"	"kindness"
— "is not jealous or boastful"	"humanity"
— "is not arrogant or rude"	"sensibility"
— "does not insist on its own way"	"generosity"
— "is not irritable or resentful"	"charity"
— "does not rejoice at wrong, but rejoices in the right"	"magnanimity"
"The greatest of these is love".	"love for others"

The parallelism is closer at some points than others,
obviously; and it is not suggested here that Smith
was consciously paraphrasing Paul. Rather, we have
here, it would seem, another illustration of how close
Smith is in much of his thinking to the Biblical approach to life.

There is nothing new, then, about the advocacy
of this principle of thought and action as the highest aspect of virtue but the relationship pattern is
both uncommon and strikingly modern. The writer
recalls vividly the exciting freshness of a lecture
in a well-known theological school some years ago
which set forth a part of this approach in terms of
Love, Law/Lust — the alliteration doubtless used to

aid students' memories — in which "love" and "law" (the equivalent of "justice", with both negative and positive aspects) are thought of as partners, not opponents, in the effort to avoid "lust" or the anarchy of irresponsible self-seeking.[17]   In Smith's thought, of course, there would be a third term — "prudence" — above the line of demarkation, just below "law", to indicate responsible concern and action for self and family — a vital and valuable addition.   This additional factor, we recall, was creatively tied in with the highest aspect of virtue by Smith when he maintained that though there is no boundary to the scope of adequately conceived goodwill, which "may embrace the immensity of the universe", yet the immediate responsibility connected with prudence remains obligatory; for "the most sublime speculation of the contemplative philosopher can scarcely compensate the neglect of the smallest active duty".[18]

Smith consistently refused to make benevolence the only true virtue for man, maintaining rather that the good life involves the combination we have been considering; for, to paraphrase St. Paul, "Benevolence cannot say to justice, I have no need of you; nor again justice to prudence, I have no need of you."[19]   In the life we are called upon to lead all three levels of attitudes and action are needed, in interpenetrative relationship and with all made effective through "self-command".   It is this latter aspect which brings the three-fold concept into active contact with the world so that we seek to act effectively not only when "there is no temptation to do otherwise" but to do so, especially, "with cool deliberation in the midst of the greatest dangers and difficulties".[20]

Another value in Smith's approach is that he regards,

we recall, the good life so conceived as "excellence, something uncommonly great and beautiful, which rises far above what is vulgar and ordinary".[21] If it is true, as one has put it, that it is infinitely worse to make virtue unattractive than to make vice attractive, Smith receives a completely clean bill of health — even more, the greatest appreciation for making the virtuous life the quintessence of the genuinely desirable.

C. Private Enterprise and Government Action

Probably the dominant impression held by most people who know anything at all about Adam Smith is that he was the father of "laissez-faire" economic theory, with self-interest linked with the pursuit of profit as the motivating force, to be given full freedom of action without governmental interference.

To claim the complete falseness of such an interpretation would be to deny or ignore much that is vital in Smith's thought, as we have seen. On the other hand, to present this as the whole of Smith's view, as has so often been done — both by proponents and by opponents of laissez-faire capitalism — is to do him the gravest injustice, as has been forcefully pointed out by Professor-Emeritus (of Economics) Charles J. Bullock of Harvard University:

> "The words italicized in this passage ('as long as he does not violate the laws of justice') are usually unnoticed or subsequently disregarded by Smith's critics who denounce 'laissez-faire' as a doctrine belonging to the days of tooth and claw, one which assumes that unrestricted pursuit of wealth is the chief end of man. This interpretation leaves out of account Smith's plain statement

that it is only so long as one 'does not violate the laws of justice' that the pursuit of self-interest is to be approved either in morals or in economics. Since he had written a whole book upon morals, he evidently did not think it necessary to enlarge upon this point in this other 'discourse' which he wrote in fulfillment of the promise he made in the last paragraph of the 'Moral Sentiments'.   But careless reading, muddled thinking, and complete misunderstanding of matters that require sustained attention and quiet reflection are so common in economics and related disciplines that they must be accepted as a matter of course. In this case, however, it is worth the visitor's attention to note, for future reference, this outstanding example of a perverted interpretation of the teachings of a great economist."[22]

The comment of Friedrich Engels toward the end of his life, in response to a question as to whether or not he and Marx had, as claimed by some interpreters, emphasized the economic factor to the exclusion of all other influences on historical development, seems especially relevant in principle in this connection:

"Marx and I are ourselves partly to blame for the fact that younger writers sometimes lay more stress on the economic side than is due to it. We had to emphasize this main principle, in opposition to our adversaries, who denied it, and we had not always the time, the place or the opportunity to allow the other elements involved in the interaction to come into their rights. But when it was a case of presenting a section of history, that is, of a practical application, the thing was different and there no error was possible. Unfortunately, however, it happens only too often that people think they have fully understood a theory and can apply it without more ado from the moment they have mastered its main principles, and those even not always correctly. And I cannot exempt many of the more recent 'Marxists' from this reproach, for the most wonderful rubbish has been produced from this quarter too."[23]

Smith, too, because of his strong opposition to the dominant mercantilism of his day, with its rigid government controls,[24] and perhaps also because of a professor's tendency to compartmentalize his thought, wrote sometimes so emphatically that it seems as if he wanted unrestrained freedom in the economic realm; but, as Professor Bullock emphasizes, the fault also lies with interpreters who have stressed one particular idea out of the context of his thought as a whole, thereby producing, in the words of Engels, "the most wonderful rubbish". Smith clearly was not undermining the "main pillar that upholds the whole edifice" of society — justice — in favor of anarchistic liberty, or its inevitable result, unrestrained monopolies (since a moral or legal vacuum would seem to lead to dictatorial consolidation of power in the economic as well as the political realm). In the words of Max Lerner, in his introduction to the "Inquiry";

> ". . . It must be said for Smith that his doctrine has been twisted in ways he would not have approved, and used for purposes and causes at which he would have been horrified."[25]

We recall, too, that in Smith's view the interest of consumers was the highest social concern[26] and that the individual should be not only protected from the injustice of others but where necessary directly served by government action — there being three general categories:

1. Protection from violence from outside the nation;

2. Protection from injustice from within the nation;

3. The carrying on of various public works and the maintenance of certain public institutions "for facilitating the commerce of society and . . . for promoting the instruction of the people."[27]

There is relatively little disagreement with Smith's thought in category #1 and increasing agreement with that in #2. It is with respect to #3, in this whole area of what might be termed societal prudence, that hot debate has developed in our time. The details of his recommendations are dated and conditioned by the specific 18th century conditions he faced; but the principles he outlined are significant in any epoch:

1. The supervision of corporations which can carry on public services profitably;[28]

2. The direct carrying on of socially useful but non-profitable functions;[29]

3. The variation of expenditures in accord with varying needs at different periods;[30]

4. The fitting of responsibility for various types of activity to suitable levels of government — national, sectional, and local;[31]

5. The raising of needed tax funds on the bases

of ability to pay, clearly known assessments, convenience of payment, and economy of collection.[32]

Thus there is responsibility plus flexibility in his approach which would seem clearly to undergird adaptability in government activity along the lines already noted — the financing out of public funds of such projects as are socially beneficial but which either cannot be, or are not being, carried out by private groups.[33]

It would seem clear, therefore, that Smith thought of there being not an alternative but a thoroughly supplementary relationship between private enterprise and government activity — the former not only allowed but encouraged within the limits of justice, the latter filling in the gaps, expanding and contracting in response to society's needs.

There is certainly no need to emphasize the contemporary relevance of such thinking.

D. International Relations

1. Spirit

Smith's fundamental cosmopolitanism is perhaps best indicated by his treatment of benevolence which, as we have seen, he regards as the highest aspect of the good life and so all-inclusive in its scope that he asserts the impossibility of conceiving of anyone outside its range.[34] And he expresses the conviction that "all the inhabitants of the universe, the meanest as well as the greatest, are under the immediate care and protection of that great, benevolent, and all-wise Being, who directs all the movements of nature, and who is determined, by his own unalterable perfections, to maintain in it at all times the greatest possible quantity

of happiness".[35] Accordingly, we recall, the wise and
virtuous man is willing to sacrifice the smaller interests
of the more limited to the larger interests of the more
inclusive, starting with his own and culminating with
those of "that great society of all sensible and intelli-
gent beings, of which God himself is the immediate
administrator and director".[36]

Of significance, too, in this connection is his choice
of a title for what has become his best known work —
his "Inquiry" being concerned not just with the economic well-being of Britain but with "the nature and
causes of the wealth of *nations*".

2. *Practice*

His opposition to tariffs for anything but strictly
revenue purposes, related to his antagonism to all
monopolies, has already been noted.[37] And even
stronger statements on the value of free trade may be
found in his writing. For example:

> "We trust with perfect security that the free-
> dom of trade, without any attention of govern-
> ment, will always supply us with the wine which
> we have occasion for; and we may trust with equal
> security that it will always supply us with all the
> gold and silver which we can afford to purchase or
> to employ . . ."[38]

Or again, the most carefully reasoned statement:

> "To give the monopoly of the home-market to
> the produce of domestic industry, in any particu-
> lar art of manufacture, is in some measure to di-
> rect private people in what manner they ought to
> employ their capitals, and must, in almost all

cases, be either a useless or a hurtful regulation.
If the produce of domestic can be brought there
as cheap as that of foreign industry, the regulation is evidently useless. If it cannot, it must
generally be hurtful. It is the maxim of every prudent master of a family, never to attempt to make
at home what it will cost him more to make than
to buy. The tailor does not attempt to make his
own shoes, but buys them of the shoemaker. The
shoemaker does not attempt to make his own
clothes, but employs a tailor. The farmer attempts
to make neither the one nor the other, but employs those different artificers. All of them find it
for their interest to employ their whole industry
in a way in which they have some advantage over
their neighbours, and to purchase with a part of its
produce, or what is the same thing, with the price
of a part of it, whatever else they have occasion
for.

"What is prudence in the conduct of every private family, can scarce be folly in that of a great
kingdom. If a foreign country can supply us with
a commodity cheaper than we ourselves can make
it, better buy it of them with some part of the produce of our own industry, employed in a way in
which we have some advantage."[39]

He admits of only two legitimate long-term excep-
tions: (1) when a particular industry is essential for
the defense of a nation it seems well "to lay some burden upon foreign, for the encouragement of domestic,
industry"; and (2) when a tax is put on a domestic
product it seems reasonable to put a like "burden" on
the same item manufactured abroad; but even these

levies, it should be noted, should not be prohibitive.
A third exception made is a short-term one, being the
granting "for a certain number of years" of exclusive
trading rights to a company undertaking to establish
a new trade "with some remote and barbarous nation"
involving exceptional risk; but after the agreed term
the field would be thrown open.[40]

Present-day efforts to reduce the trade barriers erec-
ted between nations might well be effectively strengthened by renewed study and utilization of Smith's
views and arguments.

Another striking example of Smith's ability to rise
above provincialism, and by implication above nationalism is found in his attitude with reference to the
growing tension between Great Britain and her American colonies. Publishing his views in the very year
of the American Revolution he argued for "parting
(as) good friends" instead of fighting; but what ap-
pealed to him the most was a centralized union with
representation in Parliament from all parts:

> "The assembly which deliberates and decides
> concerning the affairs of every part of the empire,
> in order to be properly informed, ought certainly
> to have representation from every part of it."[41]

He didn't underestimate the difficulties of achieving
such a goal, chief among them being "the prejudices
and opinions of the people both on this and on the
other side of the Atlantic", but he felt that no such
obstacles were insurmountable; and he thought that
the fairest principle for representation would be "in
proportion to taxation". He then proceeded to set
forth what must have been a startling idea to his
British contemporaries, that as the American colonies

grew in wealth and population they might exceed the mother country in both respects, and —

> "The seat of the empire would then naturally remove itself to that part of the empire which contributed most to the general defence and support of the whole."[42]

There would seem to be clear implications for the present in such ideas, both with reference to surviving parent-colony situations and, by natural extension, to the problems of extent and size of representation in the United Nations.

The emphasis he put in the third part of his college lectures on jurisprudence — "of all sciences by far the most important, but hitherto, perhaps, the least cultivated" — and on which he hoped to publish a major volume, is also significant in this connection.   The rules of this science he compares in importance for society, we recall, with that of the rules of grammar for composition, which he speaks of as "precise, accurate, and indispensable".[43]   All enduring nations would agree with this estimate with reference to their own internal codes of civil and criminal law; and an increasing number of concerned believers in international government are supporting as indispensable the formulation of such precise and accurate rules relating to international affairs so that the activities of individual states may be made compatible with global well-being.

A Concluding Word

Adam Smith, then, does indeed deserve to be "rediscovered" in our time, in the writer's opinion, and rediscovered fully; for far from being a conventional defender of the status quo, as so often presented, he thought in fresh and creative terms, dealing with the problems of the people of his day as a whole. And because he was concerned with "the breadth and length and heighth and depth"[44] of human life there is a timeless character about much of his thinking which makes it amazingly relevant to our country as well as his, and perhaps to any age.

Christians and non-Christians will benefit from such a rediscovery; but Christians may find special values in this approach to day by day affairs which is so permeated by an ethical concern which stems from the Judeo-Christian faith. Its being largely unknown in its ethical dimensions and hence not worn thread-bare by overmuch discussion makes it a veritable mine of thought-provoking ideas; and it is seldom unreward-ing to expose and re-expose oneself to the thought of "one of the liberators of men's minds", especially when, at a time like the present in which integration is so sorely needed in many areas of concern, the liberator is a "specialist in the relation of things".[45]

REFERENCES

[1] Recall Chapter Four, Section C. It is of interest in this connec-tion to note the words of a 20th century political economist: "Put-ting aside all details proper to an economic text-book, deep down at the root of things the essence of Smith's doctrine is semi-theological in character. It is that there is a 'Natural Order' divinely ordained. As becomes an eighteenth-century Deist brought up in Scotland, Adam Smith is somewhat shy of calling God by His name. Yet the Almighty, by whatever name He may be called, has endowed man with inclinations which have a purpose and a design." Gray, Sir Alexander, "Adam Smith", London, Published for The Historical Association by George Philip and Son, Ltd., 32 Fleet Street, General Series G. 10., p. 7.

[2] See Chapter Three, Section B. 2. a., especially the quotations with footnotes #25 and #26. Writes a 20th century economist:

"It is a very superficial view — and one which can arise only from a misreading of isolated sentences of the 'Wealth of Nations' out of their context — which suggests that for Adam Smith the individual exists apart from society and owing no duties to society. After all, Smith was quite explicit that man 'can subsist only in society' and 'was fitted by nature to that situation'." Robertson, H. M., "The Adam Smith Tradition", Oxford University Press, 1950, p. 12. It is of interest that Professor Robertson quotes the "Theory" in this connection, without even commenting on the fact, as apparently quite natural in the consideration of Smith's thought as an economist.

[3] Ibid., but limited to quotation with footnote #25.

[4] Ibid.

[5] Ibid.

[6] Ibid., quotation footnoted as #27. "The genius of Adam Smith has an even deeper lesson for the professional economist," writes Prof. W. R. Scott. "How far has the latter Adam Smith's sympathy, tolerance and the power of putting himself in the position of others? To the degree he possesses these qualities he inherits some part of the mantle of Adam Smith. In so far as he lacks them, he fails, and may fail disastrously." Scott, "Adam Smith and the City of Glasgow", Reprint from the Proceedings of the Royal Philosophical Society of Glasgow, Session 1922-1923, Volume LII, Glasgow, "The Society", 1923, pp. 139-40.

[7] See Chapter Four, Section C. 2. b., quotation with footnote #44; and Chapter Three, Section B. 2. c., quotation with footnote #40.

[8] See quotation with footnote #15 below.

[9] See Chapter Three, Section B. 2. c.

[10] Leviticus 19:18 and Luke 10:27.

[11] 1st Timothy 5:8. The idea is "Pauline" whether or not the letter as we now have it was written by Paul himself.

[12] See Chapter Three, Section B. 2. a.

[13] See Chapter Three, Section B. 2. c., quotation with footnote #40.

[14] See Chapter Two, Section B. 2., quotation with footnote #31.

[15] "The Oxford Conference (Official Report)", by J. H. Oldham, Chicago, Willett, Clark & Company, 1937, pp. 77-78.

[16] See Chapter Three, Section B. 2., quotation with footnote #43.

[17] This is based on the writer's notes on a lecture delivered by Prof. H. Richard Niebuhr at the Yale Divinity School in 1941.

[18] See Chapter Three, Section B. 2. c., quotations with footnotes #48 and #50.

[19] See 1st Corinthians 12:21 for the original from which this paraphrase is made.

[20] See Chapter Three, Section B. 2. c., quotation with footnote #53.

One is reminded here of a passage from Walter Lippmann's "A Preface to Morals", p. 3 (N. Y., The Macmillan Co., 1929), as quoted in Robert F. Davidson's "Philosophies Men Live By", N. Y., The Dryden Press, 1954, p. 177: "Because courage consists in transcending normal fears, the highest kind of courage is cold courage; that is to say, courage in which the danger has been fully realized and there is no emotional excitement to conceal the danger."

[21] Ibid., quotation with footnote #54.

[22] See Chapter Three, B. 2. h. and B. 3. b., especially the quotation with footnote #88. Bullock quotation from his "The Vanderblue Memorial Collection of Smithiana", Boston, Baker Library, Harvard Graduate School of Business Administration, 1939, p. xii. It should also be noted that "laissez-faire" is not a Smithian phrase but one made popular by the contemporary "Physiocrats" in France, whom Smith knew and admired for much of their approach; the equivalent idea appears in his thought, however, in the quotation included in Chapter Three, B. 3. b., #88 mentioned just above. Commenting on the change in connotation of the term since the 18th century, one 20th century writer says: "The term 'laissez-faire', as originally introduced, presumably by the Marquis d'Argenson, was intended as an emphatic admonition to government administrators to refrain from meddling . . . Today, the term connotes business anarchy, industry freed of all restraints of the laws of man and God. So great has been the distortion that the original sane, economic significance has been completely lost." Montgomery, George S., Jr., "The Return of Adam Smith", Caldwell, Idaho, The Caxton Printers, Ltd., 1949, p. 35.

[23] Adoratsky (Adoratskij), V., ed., "Karl Marx, Selected Works", N. Y., International Publishers, 1939, Volume 1, p. 383.

[24] Writes Max Lerner in his introduction to the Modern Library edition of "The Wealth of Nations" (op. cit.): "John Maurice Clark suggests that his system can be best understood in terms of what he was reacting against. And it is true that Smith's system of thought took its shape from his intense reaction against the elaborate apparatus of controls which the surviving feudal and mercantilist institutions were still imposing on the individual. The need for removing these controls was Smith's underlying theme." p. ix.

[25] Ibid., p. x.

[26] See Chapter Three, Section B. 3. b., quotation with footnote #90.

[27] Ibid., quotations with footnotes #92, and #93-101; also "Inquiry" (op. cit.), p. 681.

[28] "Inquiry" (op. cit.), pp. 712 ff.

[29] Ibid., p. 684.

[30] Ibid., p. 682.

[31] Ibid., p. 689.

[32] See Chapter Three, Section B. 3. b., quotation with footnote #107.

[33] Ibid., quotation with footnote #106.

[34] See Chapter Three, Section B. 2. c., quotation with footnote #48.

[35] "Theory" (op. cit.), p. 345.

[36] See Chapter Four, Section B. 2., quotation with footnote #23.

[37] See Chapter Three, Section B. 3. b., quotation with footnote #108.

[38] "Inquiry" (op. cit.), p. 404.

[39] Ibid., pp. 423-4.

[40] Ibid., pp. 429-32 and 712.

[41] Ibid., pp. 582 and 589.

[42] Ibid., pp. 589-90.

[43] See Chapter Three, Section B. 2. c., quotation with footnote #42 and "Theory" (op. cit.), p. 250. See also Isaiah 32:17 (Revised Standard Version) for the relationship of justice (or "righteousness") to peace.

[44] See Ephesians 3:18 for original of this phrase.

[45] See the end of Chapter Two, quotations with footnotes #47 and #48.

APPENDICES

Appendix #1 — Madras Conference Statement of the Christian Faith

(See Chapter Four, Section A. 2)

"We live by faith in God, the Father of our Lord Jesus Christ.

"Above all and in all and through all is the Holy Will, the Creative Purpose of the Most High. The world is His and He made it. The confusions of history are in the grasp of His manifold Wisdom. He overrules and works through the purposes of men, bringing to nought their stubborn and rebellious lust for power but building their fidelity into the structure of His Reign upon earth.

"Man is the child of God, made in His image. God has designed him for life in fellowship with Himself, and with his brothers in the family of God on earth. Yet in the mystery of the freedom which God has given him, man chooses to walk other paths, to seek other ends. He defies his Father's will. He seeks to be a law unto himself. This is the deepest cause of the evil and misery of his life. Alienated from God he seeks his salvation where it cannot be found. Impotent to save himself, he stands ever in need of conversion, of forgiveness, of regeneration.

"Who then shall save? God saves, through Jesus Christ our Lord. 'God so loved the world that He gave His only begotten Son that whosoever believeth

in Him should not perish but have everlasting life.'
This is the heart of the Christian Gospel, the Gospel
which we proclaim.

"God in His infinite love has acted for men's salvation. He has come among them in Jesus of Nazareth,
His Word made flesh. In Him, He has conquered the
power of sin and death. Jesus Christ in His teaching
and life of perfect love recalls men to that which God
would have them be, and brings them to shame for
their betrayal of His expectation. Through His faith
and perfect obedience they come to trust the only
true God. His suffering and death on Calvary bring
them to see the exceeding sinfulness of sin and assure
them of God's pardon. His resurrection is the victory of holiness and love over death and corruption.
Through His risen and living Presence, men who
dedicate their wills to Him become with Him partakers
of eternal life. In the strength and joy of forgiveness,
daily renewed at the foot of the Cross, they are made
more than conquerors over every evil.

"For Christ, the Kingdom of God was central. He
called His followers to seek first God's Kingdom and
His righteousness. Through acceptance of His call to
suffering love and through trust in divine help, men
are summoned to be co-workers with Him for the increase of justice, truth and brotherhood upon earth.
His Kingdom is both within and beyond this world.
It will be consummated in the final establishment of
His glorious reign of Love and Righteousness, when
there shall be a new heaven and a new earth where
death and sin shall be no more.

"To the gift of Christ, God has added the gift of
His Holy Spirit in the Church. Christ's true Church
is the fellowship of those whom God has called out of

darkness into His marvellous light. The guidance and power of the Spirit are given to this Church that it may continue Christ's saving work in the world. It seeks to build up its own members in the knowledge of Christ, challenging them anew with the message of his redeeming love, comforting them with the assurance of God's forgiveness in Him, teaching them the way of love through service for their brethren in Christ.

"For those that are without Christ the true Church yearns with the love of its Master and Lord. It goes forth to them with the evangel of His grace. It practices His ministry of compassion and healing. It bears witness against every iniquity and injustice in their common life. It bears their sorrows and heartache on its prayers. To it is given the solemn privilege of entering into the fellowship of the sufferings of Christ.

"In spite of all the weakness and shortcomings of our churches, Christ's true Church is within them; and our hope for the redemption of mankind centers in His work through them. Through the nurture and discipline of the Church, Christian life comes to completion; in glad service within the fellowship of the Church, Christian devotion is perfected."

— "The World Mission of the Church", N.Y., International Missionary Council, 1939, pp. 14-15.

*   *   *

Appendix #2 — The Atonement Passage from the First Edition of "The Theory of Moral Sentiments" (See Chapter Four, Section A. 2.).

"That the Deity loves virtue and hates vice, as a voluptuous man loves riches and hates poverty, not for their own sakes, but for the effects which they tend to produce; that he loves the one, only because it promotes the happiness of society, which his benevolence prompts him to desire; and that he hates the other, only because it occasions the misery of mankind, which the same divine quality renders the object of his aversion; is not the doctrine of nature, but of an artificial, though ingenious, refinement of philosophy. All our natural sentiments prompt us to believe, that as perfect virtue is supposed necessarily to appear to the Deity, as it does to us, for its own sake, and without any further view, the natural and proper object of love and reward, so must vice, of hatred and punishment.

"That the gods neither resent nor hurt, was the general maxim of all the different sects of the ancient philosophy; and if, by resenting, be understood, that violent and disorderly perturbation, which often distracts and confounds, the human breast; or if, by hurting, be understood the doing mischief wantonly, and without regard to propriety or justice, such weakness is undoubtedly unworthy of the divine perfection. But if it be meant, that vice does not appear to the Deity to be, for its own sake, the object of abhorrence and aversion, and what, for its own sake, it is fit and right should be punished, the truth of this maxim can, by no means, be so easily admitted. If we consult our natural sentiments, we are apt to fear, lest before the holiness of God, vice should appear to be more worthy of punishment than the weakness and imperfection of human virtue can ever seem to be of reward.

"Man, when about to appear before a being of infinite perfection, can feel but little confidence in his own merit, or in the imperfect propriety of his own conduct. In the presence of his fellow-creatures, he may often justly elevate himself and may often have

reason to think highly of his own character and conduct, compared to the still greater imperfection of
theirs. But the case is quite different when about to
appear before his infinite Creator. To such a being,
he can scarce imagine, that his littleness and weakness
should ever seem to be the proper object, either of
esteem or of reward. But he can easily conceive, how
the numberless violations of duty, of which he has been
guilty, should render him the proper object of aversion
and punishment; neither can he see any reason why
the divine indignation should not be let loose without
any restraint, upon so vile an insect, as he is sensible
that he himself must appear to be. If he would still
hope for happiness, he is conscious that he cannot
demand it from the justice, but that he must entreat it
from the mercy of God. Repentance, sorrow, humilia-
tion, contrition at the thought of his past conduct,
are, upon this account, the sentiments which become
him, and seem to be the only means which he has left
for appeasing the wrath which, he knows, he has justly
provoked. He even distrusts the efficacy of all these,
and naturally fears, lest the wisdom of God should not,
like the weakness of man, be prevailed upon to spare
the crime, by the most importunate lamentations of
the criminal. Some other intercession, some other
sacrifice, some other atonement, he imagines, must be
made for him, beyond what he himself is capable of
making, before the purity of the divine justice can be
reconciled to his manifold offences. The doctrines of
revelation coincide, in every respect, with those original anticipations of nature; and, as they teach us how
little we can depend upon the imperfection of our own
virtue, so they show us at the same time, that the most

powerful intercession has been made, and that the most dreadful atonement has been paid for our manifold transgressions and iniquities."

(First Edition, Part II, Section II, Chapter III, pp. 203-6.)

BIBLIOGRAPHY

Works Quoted Only

It has seemed advisable in this brief study to limit the bibliography to the list of the writings actually quoted. Many more have been consulted. For additional material the reader is referred to C. J. Bullock's "The Vanderblue Memorial Collection of Smithiana" (see below for publisher and date). Smith's own writings appear first; then come other works, listed alphabetically by names of the authors.

Writings by Smith

"The Theory of Moral Sentiments", By Adam Smith, Professor of Moral Philosophy in the University of Glasgow. First Edition, London, A. Millar, in the Strand; and A. Kincaid and J. Bell, in Edinburgh, 1759, (551 pp.).

> Smith's first important published work on the revision of which he also spent his last years.

Bohn's Standard Library Edition. London, Henry G. Bohn, 1853, (538 pp.).

> Bound with this edition, the two referred to in this study, are "A Biographical and Critical Memoir of the Author" by Dugald Stewart and "A Dissertation on the Origin of Languages" by Smith.

"An Inquiry into the Nature and Causes of the Wealth of Nations," By Adam Smith, LL.D. and F.R.S. Formerly Professor of Moral Philosophy in the

University of Glasgow. First Edition, London, printed for W. Strahan, and T. Cadell, in the Strand, 1776, (Volume 1, 510 pp.; Volume 2, 587 pp.).

Smith's second important published work and that by which he is chiefly known today.

The Modern Library Edition, New York, 1937, (976 pp.). Edited with an Introduction, Notes, Marginal Summary and Enlarged Index by Edwin Cannan, with an Introduction by Max Lerner.

The text of this edition is copied from that of the fifth, the last published before Adam Smith's death. It is the one referred to throughout this study.

Other Writings

Barnes, Harry Elmer and Becker, Howard, "Social Thought from Lore to Science; A History and Inter-pretation of Man's Ideas about Life with His Fellows". Boston, New York, etc., D. C. Heath and Company, 1938 (Volume 1, 874 pp.).

A sociology text book, with interesting summary sections on Smith (pp. 523-6 and 532-8).

Becker, Carl L., "The Heavenly City of the Eight-eenth Century Philosophers". New Haven, Yale University Press, 1932 (One of the Storrs Lectures) (168 pp.).

Lectures delivered at Yale on "Climates of Opinion", "The Laws of Nature and of Nature's God", "The New History: Philosophy Teaches by Example", and "The Uses of Posterity". Most useful for purposes of general orientation in the thought of the 18th century, with material presented in both scholarly and readable form.

Bonar, J., "The Tables Turned; A Lecture and Dia-logue on Adam Smith and the Classical Economists",

January 19, 1926.   London, P. S. King & Son, Ltd., 1926, (52 pp.).

> One of a course of lectures delivered at the London School of Economics to commemorate the 150th anniversary of the publication of "The Wealth of Nations". Contains a novel and interesting imaginary conversation between Smith, Ricardo, Mill, Marx and others in "Elysium".

Buckle, Henry Thomas, "History of Civilization in England". New York, D. Appleton and Company, 1858; (2 Volumes, 677 and 476 pp., respectively).

> Volume II, Chapter VI, of this work is "An Examination of the Scotch Intellect during the Eighteenth Century" and deals, on pages 340-60, with Adam Smith, "by far the greatest of all Scotch thinkers". The material on Hutcheson, Hume and others is also of value. Buckle's interpretations are frequently referred to by later writers.

Bullock, Charles J., "The Vanderblue Memorial Collection of Smithiana" and "A Catalogue of the Collection Presented to the Harvard Business School by Homer B. Vanderblue in Memory of his Father, Frank J. Vanderblue, and Deposited in the Kress Library of Business and Economics". Boston, Baker Library, Harvard Graduate School of Business Administration, 1939, (68 pp.). Publication Number Two of the Kress Library of Business and Economics.

> An admirable introduction, by a professor-emeritus of Economics at Harvard, not only to the catalogue of the superb Vanderblue Collection of "Smithiana" but to a study of Smith's thought as well. His emphasis, as an economist, on the importance of studying the "Theory" as well as the "Inquiry" is of special interest.

Bury, J. B., "The Idea of Progress", "An Inquiry into its Origin and Growth". New York, The Macmillan Company, 1932 (357 pp.).

Probably the best one volume treatment of the growth of the idea which has until recently had so marked an ascendancy in the conscious and unconscious thought of the modern West. An introduction by Charles A. Beard adds to its value.

Cannan, Edwin, "Lectures of Adam Smith (on Justice, Police, Revenue and Arms)". Delivered in the University of Glasgow. Reported by a student in 1763. Oxford, Clarendon Press, 1896 (293 pp.).

A carefully edited edition of an old manuscript previously unknown to the public. It supplies powerful evidence that the chief ideas of "The Wealth of Nations" were embodied in Smith's lectures prior to his contact with the French Physiocrats and their doctrines. The editor's introduction includes a table of parallel passages from the two books (the "Lectures" and "The Wealth of Nations").

Clark, J. M., Douglas, P. H., Hollander, J. H., Morrow, G. R., Palyi, M., and Viner, J., "Adam Smith, 1776-1926; Lectures to Commemorate the Sesquicentennial of the Publication of 'The Wealth of Nations'". Chicago, University of Chicago Press, 1928 (241 pp.).

An interesting collection of lectures, strong in respect, especially, to lively presentation of broad over-all views; one naturally looks to longer studies — by the lecturers themselves and others — for thorough treatment of specific issues.

Delatour, Albert, "Adam Smith: Sa Vie, Ses Travaux, Ses Doctrines". Paris, Librairie Ghillaumin et Cie., 1886 (325 pp.).

An appreciative and well-written study of Smith's life and ideas which emphasizes the relationship within a general system of the "Theory" and the "Inquiry". The author is convinced what we have in these books are but parts "d'une véritable 'Histoire de la Civilisation'" which Smith envisaged but did not complete.

Davidson, Robert F., "Philosophies Men Live By", New York, Dryden Press, 1954.

An excellent textbook for an introductory course in Philosophy built around the life and thought of some of the key personalities in philosophic history, with well-chosen quotations from original sources.

Gide, Charles, and Rist, Charles, "A History of Economic Doctrines; From the Time of the Physiocrats to the Present Day". Translated by R. Richards from 1913 edition. New York, Boston, etc., D. C. Heath and Co., 1915 (672 pp.).

One of the best surveys of modern economic thought, with a very good section on Smith — Book I, Chapter II, pp. 50-102.

Gray, Sir Alexander, "Adam Smith", London, Published for the Historical Association by George Philip and Son, Ltd., 32 Fleet Street, E.C. 4, 1948, General Series G. 10, p. 7.

The Professor of Political Economy at the University of Edinburgh stresses here the close relationship of the "Theory" and the "Inquiry" as part of his general interpretation.

Hirst, Francis W., "Adam Smith", in "English Men of Letters", edited by John Morley. New York, The Macmillan Company, 1904 (240 pp.).

A general survey of Smith's life and writings, the reason for which, after Rae's definitive work, being the discovery and issuance in 1896 of the Glasgow "Lectures". This results in certain changes of emphasis, combined with the author's own interpretations.

Mannheim Karl, "Ideology and Utopia; An Introduction to the Sociology of Knowledge". New York, Harcourt, Brace and Company, 1936 (318 pp.).

One of the volumes in the "International Library of Psychology, Philosophy, and Scientific Method", it is an able piece of work with careful documentation, including an excellent bibliography.

Marx, Karl, in "Karl Marx, Selected Works", edited by V. Adoratsky, New York, International Publishers, 1939, (Volume 1, 479 pp.).

Contains a useful selection of writings by both Marx and Engels as well as valuable biographical material on Marx.

Montgomery, George S., Jr., "The Return of Adam Smith", Caldwell, Idaho, The Caxton Printers, Ltd., 1949.

Consists largely of evaluative comments by the author.

Morrow, Glenn R., "The Ethical and Economic Theories of Adam Smith; A Study in the Social Philosophy of the Eighteenth Century". One of the Cornell Studies in Philosophy. New York, Longmans, Green, and Co., 1923 (91 pp.).

One of the most valuable studies available on the basic character of Smith's thought, with special emphasis on the relationship of the "Theory" and the "Inquiry". Eighteenth century rationalism and its opposing tendencies are discussed as well as the specific concepts employed by Smith in his two works.

Rae, John, "Life of Adam Smith". London, The Macmillan Co., 1895, (449 pp.).

Still the standard biography of Smith. It makes full use of earlier works, and subsequent studies are largely based on it — either condensing or giving supplementary details that have come to light since 1895. Scholarly and readable.

Robertson, H. M., "The Adam Smith Tradition", Oxford University Press, 1950.

In this inaugural address as Professor of Economics at the University of Cape Town, Professor Robertson quotes from the "Theory" again and again (as well, of course, as from the "Inquiry"), without any special comment — as quite natural for the treatment of Smith's thought as an economist.

Scott, W. R., "Adam Smith", (From the Proceedings of the British Academy, Volume XI). London, Humphrey Milford, Oxford University Press, 1923 (21 pp.).

Valuable as a concise interpretation by the late Adam Smith Professor of Political Economy in the University of Glasgow. It contains, also, a useful appendix on the relation of Adam Smith to the Physiocrats, with the conclusion that for "the scientific consideration of economic phenomena, the available evidence (detailed in the lecture-article) points to Adam Smith being earlier than both Quesnay and Turgot" (p. 21).

Scott, W.R., "Adam Smith as Student and Professor; With unpublished documents, including parts on the 'Edinburgh Lectures', a draft of 'The Wealth of Nations', extracts from the muniments of the University of Glasgow and correspondence". Glasgow, Jackson, Son & Company, 1937 (445 pp.).

An important supplement to Rae's biography with regard to Smith's family background and the years of his life up to 1764, when he resigned his professorship. The letters and other documents are carefully arranged and indexed. A scholarly work by one of thorough competence in the field.

Selby-Bigge, L. A. "British Moralists; Being Selections from Writers Principally of the Eighteenth Century". Edited with an Introduction and Analytical Index. Oxford, Clarendon Press, 1897 (Volume 1, 425 pp.; Volume 2, 451 pp.).

The first volume contains, following an excellent introduction, selections from the chief writings on moral questions of Shaftesbury, Hutcheson, Butler, Smith, and Bentham.

Small, Albion W., "Adam Smith and Modern Sociology". Chicago, The University of Chicago Press, 1907 (247 pp.).

An interestingly written and important book of general interpretation whose chief thesis is "that Adam Smith was fundamentally a moral philosopher, and that every division of his thinking was subordinated, in his own mind, to an inclusive moral philosophy" and that "whatever be the content of economic theory, it must find for itself a valid correlation with the whole scope of positive moral philosophy, before it can recover the relative dignity which belonged to it in Adam Smith's scheme of morality" (pp. 196-8).

Stewart, Dugald, "Account of the Life and Writings of Adam Smith, LL.D." (Read by Mr. Stewart, January 21, and March 18, 1793.) In "Transactions of the Royal Society of Edinburgh", Volume III, Part I, 1794; London, T. Cadell in the Strand, 1794, pp. 55-137. Republished on other occasions, as in conjunction with the Bohn edition of "The Theory of Moral Sentiments" of 1853, used in this study.

An account by a contemporary and friend of Smith's, valuable more as a source of information than as a literary biography — spoken of by Rae in 1895 as still "the fullest account we possess of the life of Adam Smith" (Preface).

Strong, G. B., "Adam Smith and the Eighteenth Century Concept of Progress". Chicago, University of Chicago Libraries, 1932 (70 pp.).

Various aspects of Smith's concept of social progress are considered, with emphasis on his relationship to other eighteenth century writers (especially Hume) and trends of thought.

The Bible, Revised Standard Version, New York, Thomas Nelson & Sons, 1952 (994 pp.).

"The Oxford Conference (Official Report)", by J. H. Oldham, Chicago, Willett, Clark & Company, 1937 (290 pp.).

One of the most important documents resulting from the activities of the modern "Ecumenical Movement"; the section on "The Church and the Economic Order" is of special significance.

Wilson, Woodrow, "An Old Master and Other Political Essays". New York, Charles Scribner's Sons, 1893, (181 pp.).

In the first of the essays, on Adam Smith — "An Old Master" — Wilson concentrates chiefly on Smith's forensic and literary abilities, which he considers as first-rate and describes with his usual eloquence. Emphasized, too, is the close relationship of the "Theory" and the "Inquiry".

INDEX